RYUHO OKAWA

SPIRITUAL INTERVIEW WITH THE GUARDIAN SPIRIT OF POPE FRANCIS

THE VATICAN AGONIZES OVER THE CORONAVIRUS PANDEMIC

HS PRESS

Original title: *Rome Kyoko Francis Shugorei no Reigen*
-Corona Pandemic ni yoru Vatican no Kumon o Kataru-
HS Press is an imprint of IRH Press Co., Ltd.
Tokyo
ISBN 13: 978-1-943869-84-8
ISBN 10: 1-943869-84-7
Cover Image: LucaDaviddi/shutterstock.com

No statements made by the guardian spirit of Pope Francis in this book reflect statements actually made by Pope Francis himself.

The opinions of the spirits in this book do not necessarily reflect those of Happy Science Group.
For the mechanism behind spiritual messages, see the end section.

Contents

Preface 13

PART ONE

The Pope Speaks on the Vatican's Agony Caused by the Coronavirus Pandemic

CHAPTER ONE

His Distress over Not Knowing the Will of Jesus

Spiritual Interview with the Guardian Spirit of Pope Francis

1 **The Pope's Guardian Spirit Can't Understand the Will of Jesus**

Pope Francis's guardian spirit is perplexed by Jesus's current thoughts 20

Anguish over the fact that Catholic countries have suffered massive damage from novel coronavirus infections 23

2 **Striving to Realize World Peace by Promoting Reconciliation with China**

"I want to work toward a peaceful resolution through interactions with Chinese leaders" 26

Thoughts on the tyranny and despotism of the CPC 29

"A path to peace will open if all the leaders reconcile with each other" 31

3 **Opinions on the U.S., China, and Japan**

Criticizing "America First" 35

"Chinese military expansion is for the purpose of defense" 37

The pope's opinions on Prime Minister Abe, President Trump, and President Xi Jinping 40

"The U.S. military might have released a viral weapon in Wuhan" 41

The pope's opinions on China's oppression of the Uyghurs 43

Central and South America consider the U.S. merciless 46

4 **The Pope's G.S. Emphasizes Peace and Maintaining the Status Quo over the Matter of Right and Wrong**

His checkpoints on the practice of love 48

Thoughts on current China 50

Misconceptions about the Happiness Realization Party and Yasukuni Shrine 51

The pope's guardian spirit judges Japan and China based on size 55

His thought when he arrived in Italy: "fascism has lost" 59

Prioritizing politics and economy over judging good and evil in the religious sense 60

5 **His Desire for Missionary Work in China and His Prayers to God**

The mission of the world's leading countries 62

"Wealthy countries will forget God and worship Baal instead" 64

His desire to make Communist China a country where Christianity can be spread in broad daylight 66

"I pray to God and Jesus, but I get no reply" 68

Members of Christian churches now are not very fond of religions that work miracles 71

Japan is a strange country that cannot understand the religious mind 73

6 **The Limits of His Understanding**

The pope's guardian spirit laments his lack of political influence 74

"Can't Hong Kong and Taiwan try to get along with China?" 77

"If the spiritual messages from Jesus are real, I will retire" 78

Japan should also get along with China 80

"I don't understand why Mr. Trump is trying to protect Hong Kong and Taiwan" 81

"I don't know what God is implying through the novel coronavirus infection" 83

"I just want to know the truth" 85

Does the difference in opinion come from the difference in views on international politics? 87

Can you see the world from the perspective of God and Buddha? 89

7 **The Great Savior Surpasses the Pope**

Why does Jesus come to Happy Science whose people don't pray at Saint Peter's Basilica? 92

"I can't see what Jesus thinks since I don't have the divine supernatural powers" 94

Why are his ideas different from those of Jesus? 96

It seems like God is trying to punish the U.S., too 98

"I do think Xi Jinping may be a devil" 100

"I am someone like a village chief, so I am not capable of talking about global issues" 101

"I did not realize that Japan has become a religiously developed country" 102

The pope's guardian spirit openly confesses that the Vatican's exorcisms are not effective 105

Christianity can make devils reveal their names, but can't find out the root cause of possession 108

8 **Message from the Pope's Guardian Spirit**

The message he wants to convey to Christians all over the world 110

Words of encouragement from the pope's guardian spirit 113

9 **After the Spiritual Interview** 117

CHAPTER TWO

Doubts about "Spiritual Messages from Jesus Christ"

Spiritual Interview with the Guardian Spirit of Pope Francis

1 **Background Information on the Appearance of the Pope's Guardian Spirit**

The pope's guardian spirit appeared after the author reviewed the manuscript of a spiritual message from Jesus 120

He wants to give a message to Christians 124

Will people not believe spiritual messages from Jesus, but believe spiritual messages from the pope? 129

2 **The Pope Recognizes Himself as a Politician More Than a Religious Leader**

Will the Vatican accept the contents of the recent spiritual messages from Jesus or not? 133

If the novel coronavirus is nature's fury and not a biological weapon, it can be labeled as divine punishment 138

Jesus was strong enough not to flee, even from crucifixion, but what about the pope? 141

He cannot believe that the spiritual message from Jesus is authentic 145

Appendix

Spiritual Interview with Shusaku Endo

The unexpected appearance of the spirit of Shusaku Endo 152

"Silence" is correct, so God must not speak? 154

God is a fictional figure that novelists in the past created 159

PART TWO

Finding His Character and True Thoughts

Spiritual Interview with the Guardian Spirit of Pope Francis

1 **Thoughts on Nuclear Weapons and Faith**

The guardian spirit of Pope Francis appears 166

Impressions of the film, *The Two Popes* 170

Impressions of Japan and an appeal for the abolition of nuclear weapons 171

Will Japan, which hosts U.S. military bases, be attacked by North Korea or China? 175

If Xi Jinping is going to massacre everyone, then people should abandon their faith 177

2 **Ideas Derived from the Experience of Surviving under a Military Regime**

Surviving under the Argentine military dictatorship and later becoming a pope 181

Stating reconciliation with Iran as "difficult" and referring to Iran's religious affairs 183

His answers in terms of right and wrong regarding the whole issue 188

"I want the U.S. to accept refugees" 190

Relationship with St. Francis of Assisi and Jesus Christ 193

Hope for a peaceful world without war and aversion to conflict 196

"They don't need to walk right into their own Holocaust" 198

"I did a good job of surviving without giving the enemy any excuses" 201

3 **Strong Desire to Save the Vulnerable**

"I feel that I should always be on the side of the vulnerable" 203

"America's criteria at judging the right and wrong is extremely vague" 204

"Successful Christian countries must not occupy or attack other countries out of arrogance over their success" 207

4 **Complex Feelings toward China**

Jesus's branch souls that fought against totalitarianism and communism 210

"I do not like China, but also do not hope for nuclear war between the U.S. and China" 212

"I think we need people who can express their opinions to China sternly" 214

"God would not be pleased with China's religious oppression and brainwashing" 215

Affirmation of the spread of Master Okawa's teachings 217

The direction in which the guardian spirit of Pope Francis wants people to think 218

Opinions on LGBT 219

5 **Past Life, Middle East Problems, and Views on President Trump**

"A long time ago, I came to Japan as a missionary and was caught" 221

I conveyed teachings to wartime feudal lords in Kyushu and made them Christian 223

"I came to Japan under the name of Rodrigues with Xavier" 226

Opinions about becoming the pope 228

The guardian spirit of Pope Francis remains consistently humble 230
Thoughts on Muslims and Catholics 231
Views on Israel and President Trump 233
St. Francis of Assisi and St. Clare of Assisi are far greater 236

6 **Message for Japanese People**
"I want Japanese people to help people around the world a little more" 238
Independent decision-making regarding Japanese interests 240
"I see Happy Science as a hopeful religion" 242
"Even the pope can't receive answers from Jesus in his prayers"
"Please take care of the people of the world hereafter" 244

Afterword 245

About the Author 247
What is El Cantare? 248
What is a Spiritual Message? 250
About Happy Science 254
About Happy Science Movies 258
Contact Information 260
About Happiness Realization Party 262
About IRH Press 263
Books by Ryuho Okawa 264

Preface

Truly, I feel that this year has become a year of trials and ordeals for the religious.

At the beginning of the year, it seemed as if a war would start in the Middle East due to the assassination of Iranian General Soleimani by the U.S. military. Later, in the blink of an eye, the coronavirus originating from Wuhan, China spread throughout the world, and as of this writing, millions of people have been infected and hundreds of thousands have died according to official reports.

As of today, the National Diet of Japan has decided to provide every registered resident in Japan with cash payments of ¥100,000 each, with no set date to lift the state of emergency.

In the Philippines, lockdowns in urban areas have caused unemployment and starvation among the poor, and even people affiliated with the Catholic Church, who have been volunteering their time to distribute food, have been driven away by police squads.

This book reveals the agony and suffering experienced by the guardian spirit of Pope Francis. I would like to provide this to the people of the world as a reference to form their opinion.

Ryuho Okawa
Master & CEO of Happy Science Group
May 1, 2020

PART ONE

The Pope Speaks on the Vatican's Agony Caused by the Coronavirus Pandemic

CHAPTER ONE

His Distress over Not Knowing the Will of Jesus

Spiritual Interview with the Guardian Spirit of Pope Francis

Originally recorded in Japanese on April 25, 2020, in the Special Lecture Hall of Happy Science in Japan, and later translated into English.

Francis (1936 - Present)

The 266th Roman Catholic pontiff, born as Jorge Mario Bergoglio in Buenos Aires, Argentina. Francis was elected the pope after Benedict XVI resigned in 2013. He is known to be frugal and humble. He was named "Francis" after St. Francis of Assisi, who preached poverty. Francis is a Jesuit and the first pope from Latin America.

In this book, there are a total of six interviewers from Happy Science, abbreviated as A, B, C, D, E, and F, in the order that they first appear.

1

The Pope's Guardian Spirit Can't Understand the Will of Jesus

Pope Francis's guardian spirit is perplexed by Jesus's current thoughts

RYUHO OKAWA
Well then, I would like to call His Holiness Pope Francis and have you ask him for his opinions. Today, he came to us on his own accord. Pope Francis, the 266th Pope of the Roman Catholic Church. We would like to hear your opinions.

[*About five seconds of silence.*]

POPE FRANCIS'S GUARDIAN SPIRIT
Hmm... Ah, uh...

A
Hello.

POPE'S G.S.
Ah...

A
Are you the guardian spirit of Papa (the Italian word for Pope), Pope Francis?

POPE'S G.S.
Ah, um... Soon, you are going to publish the manuscript of the spiritual messages from Jesus Christ as a book*, right? The one I saw today.

A
Yes, that's right.

POPE'S G.S.
I'm at a loss, though, because it is so different from what I think. [*Sighs.*] That's a bit of a problem.

A
What exactly is the problem?

---

* In the morning of the day of the spiritual interview, the author was reviewing *Jesus Christ's Answers to the Coronavirus Pandemic* (Tokyo: HS Press, 2020).

POPE'S G.S.
I'm planning to go to China to pray for the people of Wuhan, but that's not what Jesus said. Are we not Christians?

A
You are. It has been reported that you are planning to go to Wuhan. What message do you plan to give the world once you are there?

POPE'S G.S.
It will be similar to the prayer for the victims of the atomic bomb in Hiroshima. I want to pray for those who lost their precious lives, so that their souls may rest in peace. I will pray for world peace.

I'm wondering if that was really Jesus. [*Sighs.*] This is a problem. Jesus said China created a viral weapon and threw the world into chaos, and he made comments that seemed to imply he didn't want America or Europe to forgive China. That is different from the Jesus we believe in.

[*About five seconds of silence.*] Our Jesus does not like conflict. He does not like war. He wants peace. And he also forgives the people of China. He does not accept America because the country is so belligerent. I had always believed that this was the will of Jesus.

Anguish over the fact that Catholic countries have suffered massive damage from novel coronavirus infections

A

Of course, Jesus is praying for the weak and the poor, and working hard to save them. At the same time, he often stands up to and opposes the existing authorities. Recently, Jesus descended to Happy Science and gave us many messages about the coronavirus pandemic. As you mentioned earlier, this will be published as a book. What do you think led up to the current coronavirus pandemic?

POPE'S G.S.

Hmm, this must be a warning from God to the world; a world where people enjoy conflict and violence, and where the strong torment the weak.

A

In other words, you think that this coronavirus pandemic is a punishment from heaven to warn those in power that torment the weak. Is that right?

POPE'S G.S.
Right.

A
Now, the novel coronavirus infection that originated in China is spreading throughout the entire world. Some of the Christian countries you are guiding, Catholic ones in particular, have suffered considerable damage. Many people have been infected and many have died.

POPE'S G.S.
I don't understand why the virus came into Italy. I pray every day, so why... Jesus doesn't answer my prayers. I don't know. I don't know. I pray every day, so why are so many people dying in Italy, Spain, and France? I don't understand! I don't know, I don't know. [*Sighs.*] I don't know. God is keeping silent. I don't know.

A
I understand that you, the spirit who is now here at Happy Science, are the pope's guardian spirit. Could you tell us, within the scope of your understanding, where Pope Francis's prayers reach when he prays to Jesus, his Lord?

POPE'S G.S.
Jesus is God. I believe that God no longer listens to voices from the human world, so I was guessing the Will of God and conveying it to the people, but... [*Exhales.*] I don't understand why such a terrible thing has happened. [*Sighs.*] I don't know.

I would understand if the virus spread only in the U.S. because I think they are wrong. I wouldn't be surprised if the U.S. suffered divine punishment now. But it makes no sense for so many in Europe to suffer like this. I can't accept it. The virus is also spreading in Africa and the Middle East... I don't understand!

Also, China is the main victim, so I don't understand why everyone is blaming China, either.

2

Striving to Realize World Peace by Promoting Reconciliation with China

"I want to work toward a peaceful resolution through interactions with Chinese leaders"

B

Thank you very much for today. What makes you think that China is a victim?

POPE'S G.S.

Many pure and innocent people there were the first ones in the world to die under the attack from this unknown virus. Also, Wuhan was shut down, and its people were forced to live without freedom for two or three months. They lived through that ordeal, and need to be fully consoled now.

B

You just mentioned that China was attacked. Who do you think attacked them?

POPE'S G.S.
Countries like Japan, the U.S., and the U.K.

B
You mean, they were not attacked by Catholic countries, but by countries that follow different teachings, such as Protestantism and the Church of England? How can you be so sure about that?

POPE'S G.S.
[*Exhales.*] The number of underground Christians in China is increasing and I want to save them. I am trying to promote reconciliation with China right now, but if they fan China's hatred, I can't save the Christians there. I don't understand why they oppose each other.

A
As you just mentioned, it has been reported that there are 100 million believers in China who are active through underground churches. You said that it is your wish to save these people, but who leads the Christians in China? Is it the Roman Catholic Church, in other words, you? Or is it the bishop appointed by the Communist Party of China

(CPC)? I believe this is a very important point for the Christian faith. What are your thoughts on this issue?

POPE'S G.S.

China is not a democratic country. This is why politicians in Christian countries in the West criticize China for being wrong. However, in our view, Christianity is not a democracy, either. Christianity is structured as a hierarchy with God at the top and Jesus as the "chairman," if you will. Therefore, Christian teachings are not democratic teachings. So, I think it is wrong to use democracy alone as the basis for determining whether or not a belief is heretical or evil.

A

Roman Catholicism places God at the top, as do other religions, and on that point, I agree. The question, however, is this: "Who conveys the voice of God? Is it the Pope, who is the head of the church, or the CPC, which is materialistic and atheistic, meaning it denies religious faith?"

In China, President Xi Jinping is like the pope, and I suspect he is trying to control the religious believers as he wants. What are your views on this situation?

POPE'S G.S.

Xi Jinping is probably the "god of China." He is going to make 1.4 billion people in the country his believers. However, the country also contains Christians who, I'm sure, are torn between whether to obey orders from Xi Jinping or follow the teachings of the Christian God. I want to work toward a peaceful resolution through interactions with Chinese leaders, but this is difficult because Protestant countries in the West consider China an enemy and also because I can't get Japan to act since Christians in Japan have very little political power.

Thoughts on the tyranny and despotism of the CPC

A

What do you think of President Xi Jinping? Do you think he hears the words of God or Jesus?

POPE'S G.S.

Hmm... I don't know. His country suffered bombings, invasions, plunderings, and assaults by the Japanese army during WWII. Yet, they succeeded in carrying out major development as you see now. I think that suggests a good amount of effort and love for the people.

A
Very soon, the CPC will mark the 100th year since its establishment. Also, more than 70 years have passed since the founding of the People's Republic of China. During those years, many pure and innocent Chinese citizens have been killed due to the tyranny and despotism of the CPC. Are you aware of that?

POPE'S G.S.
Similarly, Christians were persecuted by the Roman Empire during the first 300 or so years of Christianity. A great number of believers were fed to lions. Many, many of them were stoned to death, crucified upside down, run through with spears, or slashed to death.

But this does not mean we hate the historic Roman Empire. It prospered for 1,000 years, East and West Empires, so I'm sure it was part of God's plan. What happened was just a series of unfortunate incidents occurring due to differences in people's ethnicities and differences in opinions between national leaders. I believe so. So, the Christians who were killed and the soldiers in the Roman Empire who persecuted them were both blessed by God.

Considering this, the persecution by modern China still does not seem as cruel as the one-sided killing of Christians by the Roman Empire. It's true that over the last 70 years, a lot of people have died due to food shortages and various other causes, but Mao Zedong and those under him were probably very sad about this. Then, Deng Xiaoping came along and ensured everyone had enough food. Later, the current leaders appeared and they achieved enough economic growth to put them on par with and even surpass the West. They even surpassed Japan. They were able to pull ahead of Japan, a country that had once trampled on them. I don't think any of this would have been possible without God's blessing.

"A path to peace will open if all the leaders reconcile with each other"

B

I can clearly see that you have strong feelings for the believers in China. Do you think saving the Christians in

China requires you to first speak with the CPC if you want to secure their safety? Do you think Chinese Catholics will be happy as long as they can live long?

POPE'S G.S.
[*Exhales.*] People are happy if they can live in peace. That's important. I believe my mission is to prevent the people living in this world from being killed through torture, suffering, or starvation just for believing in Christianity.

A
Specifically, what are you hoping to do?

POPE'S G.S.
I want to develop mutual understanding with Chinese leaders.

A
I, too, hope that China and Catholicism, namely the Vatican, can find a peaceful resolution. However, the CPC leaders deny religious faith. Do you think it will be possible to truly reconcile with the leaders of CPC, considering they deny faith?

POPE'S G.S.
There are many Christians among the pro-democracy group in Hong Kong and the Hong Kong government that is oppressing them. Since last year or over the last several years, there have been repeated instances of suppression and resistance among Christians. This is rarely seen in history. In other words, some force is working on Christians to make them hate each other. This might come from China's policy that aims to make Mr. Xi Jinping's ability to unify, lead, and act stronger.

Not only do I portray myself as a religious figure to the world, but also as a political one. Even so, not many people listen to me, despite my position. People may listen to me when I speak, but they aren't moved to action.

Politics and religion have a difficult relationship. I am sure there are many Christians aboard U.S. aircraft carriers, but they don't follow what I say. They follow the orders of their president. Everyone has their own lot in the world like that, so it's difficult for people to disobey the actual laws and commands that maintain political order. Also, no one can guess the Will of God, so I am trying very hard to interpret it the best I can. Anyway, I just feel that a path to peace will open if all the leaders reconcile with each other.

As for the Jesus Christ you speak of, I think he is one aspect of a large spiritual energy form named "Jesus Christ." To me, what he is saying sounds more like Yahweh, the "judging god," and less like the reconciling god that we believe in.

3
Opinions on the U.S., China, and Japan

Criticizing "America First"

B
As I listen to you, I can tell that you place importance on reconciliation and that you consider it to be peace. However, this could lead to just maintaining the status quo, meaning the situation will never change. My understanding is that in early Christianity, followers learned the teachings of Jesus and then preached the Gospel through their faith in God, but they sometimes came into conflict with the authorities at the time. But even so, Christians have worked hard to create the Kingdom of God. What do you think about the missionary work of believers?

POPE'S G.S.
If you go back to the starting point, all we can believe in are the words and actions of Jesus as recorded in the Bible. That's why I told President Trump that God wants us to build bridges, not walls. Maybe it's because he was trying to build a wall that the virus went over it and spread around

the world. Once people in other countries imitated the "America First" attitude, the virus went over the wall and spread throughout the world. This is God's punishment, don't you think?

There are also devils in politics. Trump is a devil. This virus out of China might be a way of destroying the rule of devils.

B

We, too, feel that the novel coronavirus pandemic is one of God's punishments, but it is also affecting Italy, the very center of Catholicism. We think this might be God's way of conveying some sort of message. What do you think?

POPE'S G.S.

It's important to value your neighbors and to avoid fighting with, hating, or shooting your neighbors. Those sorts of things go against the Will of God. The "America First" idea is wrong because the U.S. has an obligation to help starving countries.

I grew up in South America. I lived there and conducted missionary work there. So, I am well aware of how much the U.S. has abandoned and harmed those impoverished countries. If the U.S. is just following in the footsteps of what Europe did in the past, then both Europe and the U.S. need to deeply reflect on that. I believe they should learn from the mentality of Asia, which has long been seeking for peace.

"Chinese military expansion is for the purpose of defense"

A
I understand that forgiveness, reconciliation, and peace are extremely important values in Christianity. However, I also think that, from the perspective of God or Jesus, there is an objective sense of justice, namely, what is right and what is wrong. What are your thoughts on justice?

POPE'S G.S.
[*Exhales.*] When it comes to righteousness and justice, Trump is neither righteous nor just. Japanese Prime Minister Abe is also extremely aggressive. He is trying to create a totalitarian country. He is trying to pull Japan into war again, this time WWIII. That's why I visited Japan

last year (2019) and warned the Christians in Japan to be careful. I recommended them to defang and declaw Japan, so that it can be a peaceful country and that it will never again cause war like they did in WWII.

There is no need for nuclear weapons. Japan doesn't need to have those, and I think the countries that have them should be ashamed of themselves. To me, justice means, "God will not allow us to use things like nuclear weapons, aircraft carriers, missiles, and submarines to unilaterally attack weaker countries."

A

In terms of military power, specifically, numbers of soldiers and weapons, China surpasses Japan by far. Also, as this coronavirus pandemic is now shaking up the world, publications like the American newspaper *Wall Street Journal* have even reported that China secretly conducted underground nuclear experiments last year.

China is trying to invade neighboring countries using its military might, including nuclear weapons, aircraft carriers, missiles, and submarines, and is also trying to put other countries under control through its military power. Are you willing to allow such an approach by China?

POPE'S G.S.
China might have become a military power, but they aren't yet strong enough to defeat the U.S.-Japan alliance. So, I think China's military strength is for the purpose of defense. I don't agree with North Korea launching missiles, but considering 90 percent of its citizens are starving, we must help them in some way while upholding their honor.

Japan is looking for a reason or pretense to re-militarize itself. But then again, there are people like that everywhere. This seems like the same path taken by Hitler and Mussolini.

China is strengthening its defenses, but over the last 2,000 years, it has rarely invaded and controlled another country.* China doesn't seem to have done anything like what European countries did. I think China is mainly just improving its ability to defend its 1.4 billion citizens.

* The statement about Chinese history made by the guardian spirit of Pope Francis is different from historical facts. In the past, China often invaded and ruled other countries. For example, during the Yuan dynasty, China invaded Poland and Hungary. More recently, China has invaded Inner Mongolia, East Turkistan (Uyghur), and Tibet in the 20th century and is now ruling them as autonomous regions.

The pope's opinions on Prime Minister Abe, President Trump, and President Xi Jinping

A

I would like to reconfirm your opinion on something you mentioned a moment ago. Do you mean that, to you, Japanese Prime Minister Abe and U.S. President Trump look like Hitler and Mussolini during WWII?

POPE'S G.S.

Yes. They seem exactly the same. That's how they appear. They seem to want to recreate their nations to be more militant and warlike, all by themselves, through a single administration.

A

Then, what do you think of Mr. Xi Jinping?

POPE'S G.S.

Hmm... I think he is strengthening China's defensive and economic capabilities because he fears that the nation will soon be attacked by the U.S. And I think he is trying to protect freedom of navigation in the seas of Asia from the threat of the U.S. Navy's Seventh Fleet.

The U.S. was somewhat justified during WWII, but I disagree with every war by them since the Vietnam War. It was just an invasion by stronger countries. Also, both the Iraq War and the war that is about to break out in Iran are the results of the American aggressive way of thinking.

Through the One Belt One Road Initiative, China is trying to create world peace by connecting the countries in the Middle East, Africa, and Europe. I think this is a very important thing to do. This will help protect countries in the Middle East and Africa from U.S. attacks.

"The U.S. military might have released a viral weapon in Wuhan"

B

You just mentioned that you think the alliance between Japan and the U.S. is superior to the power of China. Does that mean you think the most important thing right now is to side with China, which is less strong, to prevent conflict?

POPE'S G.S.

I don't believe it, but let's assume, as you say, the coronavirus was developed as a weapon in a virology institute in Wuhan,

China, and leaked from there. If so, I believe this is because China thinks it can't defend itself against the U.S. without developing such a virus, as China is in an inferior position.

It could also be possible that the U.S. military released a viral weapon in Wuhan, as China claims. It is a known fact throughout the world that the U.S. developed bacteriological weapons, including viruses, for practical use. They want to experiment with these somewhere.

The U.S. is capable of taking military action anywhere in the world within 24 hours, so they should be capable of attacking from outer space.

A

I am sure the U.S. has taken measures that enable them to launch military operations anywhere in the world. President Trump is pressuring Iran to shift to more democratic political systems by projecting American military power, but it seems to me that he is extremely careful regarding taking actual military actions.

POPE'S G.S.

I don't think so. It was Mr. Trump who launched missiles at Syria while Mr. Xi Jinping was visiting the U.S., and it was the U.S. who attacked Iranian General Soleimani using a drone when he was on an inspection visit to Iraq in January. That's how they operate; they attack without notice. So, if there is military destruction without any prior indications, it makes the most sense to think the U.S. did it.

I can't read leaders' minds, so maybe all leaders think similarly, but he is the kind of guy who talks about ridiculous things like building a wall along the Mexican border to keep out poor immigrants from Mexico. If he isn't labeled a racist, then who is?

I do not think that a person who is trying to build a wall to keep out Mexicans, who are supposed to be neighbors and friends, has any hesitations in killing Chinese people, who are the yellow race.

The pope's opinions on China's oppression of the Uyghurs

B

You mentioned earlier that China might be developing biological weapons because it is in an inferior position. However, in addition to the oppression of Christianity, the CPC government, which you think is in an inferior position, is actually intensifying its crackdowns in Inner

Mongolia, Uyghur, and Tibet by building concentration camps and through other means. Their actions do not appear to be acts of "loving your neighbors" at all. Yet, you don't think it can be helped because the CPC government is in an inferior position. Is that right?

POPE'S G.S.

The area where the Uyghur people live has been incorporated into China as an autonomous region, but people there continued staging coup d'états against the central government all through the year, so they would be massacred if there were no concentration camps for political criminals. I can understand that. Looking back on the long history of China, it was the Uyghurs who came to attack China from the other side of the Great Wall. So, if China were to grant them full autonomy again under Islam, they would just arm themselves and turn into a force that could throw the country into chaos. There is no way China will let that happen, so it is only natural for the Chinese government to keep them under surveillance and watch what they do. It also makes sense that they are forced to read and speak Chinese and receive occupational training.

If Uyghurs are right, then other Islamic countries would have to stand up in cooperation to help them. But the fact that they have been completely abandoned probably means there is some reason that keeps them from receiving support even under the name of religious faith.

A

From another perspective, you can see that the Islamic Middle East has a very close economic relationship with China through the One Belt One Road Initiative you just mentioned. So, if those countries were to show their willingness to fight China in the name of Islam to protect the Uyghur Autonomous Region, where many Muslims live, then instead, China could shake them up using economic tools.

Therefore, Islamic countries can't freely support or help the Uyghurs because they have become economically dependent on China. The reason is not that they think the Uyghur faith is a problem.

POPE'S G.S.

I don't know much about that, but Happy Science has also been campaigning a lot against China's oppression. You seem to support the movement to free the Uyghur Autonomous Region. Hmm... The only country that showed some agreement is Turkey.

As for the number of viral infections, Turkey has surpassed Iran and now has the most cases of infected people in the Islamic world. Many people are going to die from the virus in these two powerful countries, Turkey and Iran.

Central and South America consider the U.S. merciless

POPE'S G.S.
Hmm… I don't really know what's right, but we only saw the U.S. to be merciless. They thought only about making South and Central America poor. We even refused to study English because we thought that, if we learned it, we would be incorporated into the U.S. So, maybe the Uyghurs are refusing to learn Chinese for the same reason or another.

Then again, it is the Beijing government that is building highways from inland China all the way to the Uyghur region, building skyscrapers, and creating jobs. Under the Beijing government's planned economy, Uyghurs can work and make money to live, but they seem to lack gratitude for that. Instead of expressing gratitude, all they talk about is faith, but I get the feeling that it is just an excuse for them to rebel.

South America is also a part of the Christian world, but it does not necessarily mean people in South America should hate North America where the population is mostly Protestant, just because they are Catholic. There are Catholics in the U.S., too. There was even a Catholic president, was it Kennedy? So, there is no religious conflict. But in South America and up to Mexico, a lot of people are anti-American. The American way is to take as many things as possible away and consume those things themselves. They have no intention of making the regions they exploited richer. They leave those countries impoverished, so they are no different from Spain and Portugal during the colonial period.

Looking back on the imperialistic rule that lasted for 500 years, we cannot help but harshly criticize the U.S. we see today.

4

The Pope's G.S. Emphasizes Peace and Maintaining the Status Quo over the Matter of Right and Wrong

His checkpoints on the practice of love

B

You made a comment comparing the U.S. now with the moves of Spain and Portugal during the so-called Age of Discovery. Back then, the teachings of Catholicism spread throughout the world. Why couldn't the teachings of Catholicism stop imperial colonization? What are your thoughts on that?

POPE'S G.S.

At that time, we thought spreading Christian culture throughout Asia and South America would help enlighten people there because they were really primitive, as far as we could see. However, we also needed political power because we, as a religion, lacked the ability to convey our teachings. So, I think the Age of Discovery came when our desire to spread the teachings were combined with the political desire to obtain resources through trade or the desire to gain ports and other things. At the time, it was considered good for Christianity to spread to the end of the world. As a result, military troops committed cruel acts in many places, which I believe was a sad thing.

On the other hand, however, it is also true that missionaries who traveled to Central and South America were attacked and killed, one after another, by local religions and chiefs. Some were crucified and thrown into the river. So, in that sense, both sides had very mixed feelings.

When Christianity spread in Japan, it spread among feudal lords to some extent. But the *bakufu* (feudal government) oppressed Christianity and killed almost all the Christians. Many people secretly kept their faith as hidden Christians for several hundred years. Also, an atomic bomb was dropped on Nagasaki, where many hidden Christians lived, so they suffered double the tragedy.

Religion has had its bright and dark sides, so I don't really know, but basically, I think giving first priority to peace is the checkpoint for determining whether or not you are practicing love. Once in a while, it can be a good and just choice to push your own ideas onto others than to put peace first, but this could sometimes lead to a disaster.

The U.S. is the only country to ever drop atomic bombs

on humanity. I don't agree with the idea of Japan, a victim of atomic bombs, threatening their neighbors with nuclear bombs. Hmm... But I agree with the idea of contributing to world peace.

I believe that, as history continues to unfold, the world will head toward a bipolar order with the U.S. on one side and China on the other. So, there needs to be a balance of power between these two nations.

Thoughts on current China

B

According to your opinion, the status quo will be kept by balancing the power between the U.S. and China and thereby preventing conflicts. Will the souls of Catholics living under the CPC regime be saved in the current situation? What does it mean to save their souls?

POPE'S G.S.

I don't know. I have no idea, but looking at the history of China, they think if the regime just torments its people through oppression, a revolution will break out and overthrow the regime. They have a concept called *Ekisei* revolution (a revolution decreed by heaven).

However, more Chinese people are happy to see that their country has achieved growth and development compared to those who are suppressed and want to overthrow the regime. The country has become wealthy and quite many Chinese people have moved out of China. Instead of being envious, everyone should simply be happy about China's success. Being happy about it would justify all those young Americans who fought the Japanese army at the cost of their lives. If you do not approve of China's success, then the victory of the U.S. forces ever since they defeated the Japanese forces (during WWII), even before the Vietnam War, would be wrong. But history has not approved this yet.

Misconceptions about the Happiness Realization Party and Yasukuni Shrine

B

I agree that you cannot see the great flow of history in a short span. I am sure we will encounter many things that are too difficult and complicated to understand as we foresee what may happen in the world from now on.

To me, it sounds like you are saying that you want to maintain the status quo while you are alive because you do not understand, and that this is what peace is all about. What is your actual intention?

POPE'S G.S.

Hmm... In fact, I think Mr. Obama is right. The U.S. should first issue a nuclear-free declaration and reduce their military capabilities and the rest of the world should also join that effort. It appears unlikely for China to let go of their hundreds of nuclear weapons unless the U.S. and Russia take the initiative to promote denuclearization. The U.S. and Russia already have thousands of those weapons. Unless those two countries reduce their stockpiles, I don't think it will be possible to denuclearize China.

So, I understand Japan is in a very difficult position, but Japan should give up on the idea of using militarism to open a path for themselves. The Happiness Realization Party (HRP) is holding a convention now*, right? I hear that the HRP advocates a revival of militarism and cannot

* "The 11th-anniversary convention of the Happiness Realization Party" was held on April 25, 2020, the day this session was recorded.

gain public support at all. So, there might be something wrong with your ideas.

A
I would like to correct your misunderstanding. The HRP is in no way a party that advocates the rebirth of militarism. Actually, over the 70-plus years since the end of WWII, Japan hasn't had sufficient defense capabilities. This is why Japan is facing a security threat posed by China and North Korea and the people are living in fear. So, the HRP is insisting that Japan needs to possess defense capabilities in a just manner and that the Japanese people have to defend their country on their own. The HRP is not saying Japan should attack China and North Korea using military forces.

POPE'S G.S.
But I heard the party leader sheds tears whenever she visits Yasukuni Shrine. That shows that the party is trying to revive militarism. Even the leader of the Liberal Democratic Party (LDP) cannot visit the shrine now, but the leader and other members of the HRP visit Yasukuni Shrine. It sounds like the party is full of militarism. I hear that's the reason the party cannot win votes.

A

I would like to correct your remarks about that, too. First of all, Western countries regard Yasukuni Shrine as a place that enshrines the souls of aggressors...

POPE'S G.S.

It's a "war shrine," isn't it?

A

Sure, it is sometimes called a war shrine, but frankly speaking, it enshrines and consoles the spirits of soldiers who fought and died in WWII. It is in no way a symbol of militarism dedicated to aggressors.

POPE'S G.S.

You're regarding those who fought as heroes.

A

That also applies to the U.S. and European countries, not only Japan. It is completely natural to praise soldiers who fought to protect their fellow people as heroes and for citizens to mourn their deaths and console their spirits. So, it is wrong to brand only Japan as militaristic.

POPE'S G.S.

I don't think it's natural at all. Even the souls of soldiers who invaded China have been enshrined, so China cannot keep quiet about that.

A

That is exactly why Prime Minister Abe cannot visit Yasukuni Shrine now. But as for this, the faith a Japanese prime minister has and the religious facilities he worships at are internal affairs, so it's none of the other countries' business.

The pope's guardian spirit judges Japan and China based on size

POPE'S G.S.

Hmm... It is said that Japan invaded Okinawa and took it from China.

A

Okinawa was never a part of Chinese territory. Historically, during the Edo period, the Satsuma Domain conquered and ruled the Ryukyu dynasty, and the Meiji government carried out the so-called Ryukyu annexation and established Okinawa Prefecture. I know this has provoked different emotions among the people of Okinawa, but the government at the time did that, not because they wanted to exploit people in Okinawa like what Western countries did under their colonial rule, but because they aimed to modernize Okinawa and help the people there enjoy happy lives.

POPE'S G.S.
According to my limited knowledge, the Satsuma Domain ruled the Ryukyu dynasty to force the dynasty into offering their valuables as tribute. Hmm... I guess there are many different ways to look at it.

Geopolitically, though, China is a massive country. China is 20 times the size of Japan, with a population roughly 10 times larger. It is natural for Japan to be under China's protection.

B
Then, let me ask you instead: Do you think Okinawa should be protected by China, not Japan, because Japan is a small country?

POPE'S G.S.

Hmm... If Japan, a country one-tenth the size of China, were to decide to invade China like they once did, I think there would be quite a number of problems.

A

Japanese people nowadays have no intention of invading China.

POPE'S G.S.

Japan should convey to the nuclear powers the tragedies of the use of atomic bombs in Hiroshima and Nagasaki and urge them to give up nuclear weapons. This is the ideal of Japanese diplomacy. I believe it is the Japanese government's duty to campaign for eliminating nuclear capability itself from the world as the country that experienced the nuclear power plant accident in the Great East Japan Earthquake and the following radioactive contamination.

B

As for your understanding of history, Japan has also been attacked by China several times...

POPE'S G.S.
Oh...

B
Historically, many things have happened between the two countries...

POPE'S G.S.
Japanese people are the descendants of the Chinese who moved to this island, right?

B
In terms of language, there was an ancient Japanese language. It is also said that there was a civilization unique to Japan.

POPE'S G.S.
They used Chinese characters, though. I heard that Chinese culture enlightened the Japanese people.

B
Yes, Chinese characters were introduced to Japan, but even before that, there was an ancient Japanese writing system called *Hotsuma* letters.

His thought when he arrived in Italy: "fascism has lost"

B

Please excuse me for saying this. It seems to me that you have heard quite pro-Chinese opinions. Is someone advising you regarding your understanding of history?

POPE'S G.S.

Hmm... I was in Argentina for a long time and suddenly elected pope, so I find some things difficult to understand. I think my experiences have an influence on my limited understanding.

When I arrived in Italy, what I thought was, "fascism has lost." We should never have a political leader, who gains overnight popularity among the people but is hanged to death after he is defeated, to come to power again. So, as far as the Christian church or the Vatican is concerned, I think we need to continue conveying the message of peace to the world as much as possible in order to prevent such a militaristic dictator from ever gaining power again.

So, it seems to you the majority of Japanese Christians are left-wing. You probably think their pacifism is fake, but it might be the only path to survival. Italy never wants to experience what they did again, so they need to adopt the creed not to fight. That's also why the EU was formed.

Seeing Italy's predicament, China tried to provide economic assistance and even dispatched medical care teams amidst the panic caused by the coronavirus. Hmm... I don't know why you and I see things so differently. Why are we so different?

Prioritizing politics and economy over judging good and evil in the religious sense

B
The situation could turn for the better, but it could also turn for the worse, of course. Are you concerned about the situation changing? Do you not want that to happen?

POPE'S G.S.
Hmm...

B
You pointed out that the U.S. is a very dictatorial country, but even Argentina, your home country, worked on economic reform based on American advice. In fact,

many countries in South America have adopted economic policies that worked well in the U.S. Also, President Trump announced that the U.S. will send ventilators to Central and South American countries despite the U.S. also facing supply shortages due to the coronavirus pandemic.

I get the feeling you are overly concerned about changing the status quo.

POPE'S G.S.

Hmm... I'm not sure about that. The U.S. has caused a lot of damage to the economies of countries such as Argentina, Brazil, Honduras, and Ecuador. Many countries in Latin America are upset by inflation and so on, reducing their currencies to nothing more than slips of paper. Violence is rampant and guns are everywhere, so there is nothing good about American culture. Christianity cannot fight against this using the Cross anymore. There is nothing that can be done until those countries improve politically and economically.

They are stuck unless everything about their politics improves a little, instead of trying to subdue evil in a religious sense. Fundamentally, we must not welcome those who disrespect people in less developed nations.

5

His Desire for Missionary Work in China and His Prayers to God

The mission of the world's leading countries

B

You will be met with strong resistance whenever you try to push privatization in an economy centered on state-run companies. That's what happened in Argentina and its neighbor, Chile. There have been cases in history when economies grew by bringing out the power of private sectors.

POPE'S G.S.

Few people now want to immigrate to Argentina or Chile. In the past, a large number of Japanese people immigrated to Brazil, but I'm sure no one now would say they want to immigrate to Brazil because it's not an easy country to live in.

The U.S. alone has many citizens who are 100 times wealthier than people in poor nations, so it makes perfect sense for tons of illegal or "hidden" immigrants to make their way into the country. Therefore, if the U.S. wants to stop these hidden immigrants from coming in, they need to help the immigrants' homelands improve their security and stabilize their economies.

As the world's leading nation, the U.S. should be trying to use wisdom to solve those problems. Instead, all they are thinking about is strengthening their military power and crushing the second and third ranked countries that threaten their dominance. That's why I teach that what the U.S. is doing is not in accordance with the will of Jesus. Am I wrong?

A

As you just mentioned, people who come into the U.S. illegally through Mexico commit crimes like drug trafficking and threatening the lives, safety, and property of Americans, so the U.S. is trying to protect...

POPE'S G.S.

Some people may see it that way, but isn't it the mission of the world's leading nation to think about what it can do to improve the standard of living of people in countries where the only way they can make money is by bringing drugs into the U.S., even though they are fully aware that it is illegal?

"Wealthy countries will forget God and worship Baal instead"

A

From that perspective, the most important thing is for the political and economic system to work properly in the immigrants' home countries. It is unfortunate for people to have to flee from countries in which they were born and raised. Politicians in each country should think about how they can help such people live happily in their beloved homeland.

At first, the idea of "America First" or the idea of putting one's own country first by President Trump might seem like an extremely self-centered assertion, but actually, it might be the best path for the people of that country.

POPE'S G.S.

The number of Muslims in the U.S. is also rapidly increasing. Many Muslims are entering the country. I'm hoping the U.S. isn't that intolerant, but discrimination and oppression of Muslims have gotten a lot worse there. There were the 9/11 terrorist attacks, which I'm sure are a factor. That plays a part. It is also a fact that many Hispanics have immigrated to the U.S. since 20 percent of people in America understand Spanish.

At any rate, though, if leaving your own country makes you poorer, then you will not leave. But if there is a country where people earn tens of times or even 100 times more than you do in your own country, you will probably want to go there and learn.

Japan is somewhat like that. The per-capita income in Japan is as much as 100 times greater than that of the poorer countries in Asia, but Japan is very strict on immigration. It is a "closed" country. I feel that Japan thinks in a narrow way or is narrow-minded despite being a first-rate country. Japan has already adopted a "Japan First" policy. It tends to be domestically-oriented. Japan should think more about their mission.

B

So, do you think countries that have become affluent must give everything to poor countries to make everyone equal? Do you think countries that are on their way to becoming wealthy should become rich, not on their own, but by having wealth donated to them?

POPE'S G.S.

Wealthy countries forget God. They may think they believe in God, but somewhere along the way, they come to believe in a devil. Their faith changes into the belief in Baal*. At some point, their faith changes from the belief in Jesus to the belief in Baal without them realizing it. They don't know exactly at what point this happens, though. They just keep aiming higher and higher. Germany failed in this way and so did Japan. I believe the U.S. will follow the same path.

His desire to make Communist China a country where Christianity can be spread in broad daylight

B

I am aware there is a danger that some people think only about worldly affluence. In your opinion, what is an ideal wealthy country?

---

* A materialistic and mammonist worshiping belief that was popular around ancient Middle East. Baal is believed to be the same being as the devil Beelzebub (Belial). The Old Testament describes that the prophet Elijah, who preached that only Yahweh should be worshiped as God, confronted the prophets of Baal and won.

POPE'S G.S.
I don't think Communist China, which is materialistic and atheistic, is an ideal country at all, as you seem to think I do. There is no way I would consider it ideal.

The People's Republic of China (PRC) was founded in 1949, so it has only been around for 70 years. Over those 70 years, their way of life has considerably improved compared to what it used to be. They have also constructed plenty of skyscrapers in their major cities along the Pacific coast. They have achieved extraordinary economic development. They profess themselves to be a materialistic and atheistic communist nation, but economically, they are about to join the Free World.

If we can overturn their system through Christian missionary work and convert the economically wealthy country of 1.4 billion people into a Christian country, it can transform from hell into heaven. That's why I am trying, within the limit of my poor faculties, to spread Christianity in China, not by denying them, but by accepting and embracing them.

However, Mr. Trump is trying to crush the annoying China because the no. 2 country is trying to become no. 1. This will just bring hatred only. So, we think differently.

B
Do you want to convert the CPC into a Christian regime?

POPE'S G.S.
Yes, I do. I want to make China a country where you can conduct missionary work in broad daylight.

In that sense, it wouldn't be so bad for countries like Italy, France, and Spain to deepen their relationship with China. I hope that I will be able to convert a country of 1.4 billion people to Catholicism. I pray to God for this, but it will be hard to achieve in reality.

As you mentioned, the underground Christians in China are under the surveillance and protective supervision of Beijing authorities. In general, they see Christianity as an evil religion and I often hear about people who suddenly disappear, only to be found dead sometime later. So, unless I build a connection, no one can protect or save those people.

"I pray to God and Jesus, but I get no reply"

POPE'S G.S.
Imagine if I were to enter Wuhan saying, "You are the ones who created the coronavirus and threw the world into the

hell of fear!" They would surely see me as an enemy and reject me. Instead, I will tell them I want to hold a memorial service for those who died in Wuhan because there were also Christians among them. That's the way I want to do things.

I don't know if you and I think so differently, but the words of Jesus that have come through you are different from not only my views, but also from the traditional views of the Vatican. I can't tell whether it is really Jesus or a devil, or whether the faith unique to Japan called Happy Science is about to be established.

Looking at you, I don't think you look so cruel, though. Hmm...

B

You said you want to do missionary work in China as well, but you transferred the right to appoint church bishops to the CPC government. Do you think you can save Chinese people by continuing to deepen your relationship with China and visiting Wuhan to reconcile with them?

POPE'S G.S.

They might have control over the political system, but as long as Christianity survives in China, the Christians there will have to continue reading the Bible, so Christian ideas are sure to spread. Right now, Christians have to hide themselves, but I want to do my best to enable them to be more open about their religion.

So, I am trying to urge China to have a better understanding by keeping the U.S. in check.

B

In reality, though, don't you feel you have reached the limit of what you can do and have no idea what to do?

POPE'S G.S.

I have my limits, so I pray every day. I get down on all fours and pray to God and Jesus, like Buddhist people and people of some religions do, but I have gotten no reply. None at all. I get no answer no matter how much I, the pope, pray.

I don't understand. Why don't I get any answer even though I'm trying to spread Christianity, but Jesus descends to Happy Science, where the members don't believe much in Christianity, and tries to preach the Gospel? I don't know.

A

According to Happy Science teachings, the being who guided Jesus when he was alive or the one he called his

"Heavenly Father" is now living as Master Ryuho Okawa of Happy Science. So, Jesus supports us based on this connection.

POPE'S G.S.
You might think so, but we in the Christian world will never be able to understand that.

Members of Christian churches now are not very fond of religions that work miracles

B
Jesus really cares about those who gather at churches. He recently gave us a powerful message in the form of a spiritual message. He said he wants the Christian world to look at the activities and the miracles of Happy Science and to awaken to their true purpose. This showed Jesus's deep love for Christians.

POPE'S G.S.
It's sad, but members of Christian churches now are not very fond of religions that work miracles. When such religions appear, they immediately label those as workings

of the devil. They start calling them heretical and labeling them cults.

In reality, they teach based only on theology and do not readily accept religions that work miracles.

B

However, you want to save the underground Christians in China who are part of a population of 1.4 billion. Doesn't that mean you are hoping for a miracle?

POPE'S G.S.

I believe even Mr. Xi Jinping is somewhat afraid of Mr. Trump. So, he thinks having the pope on his side will benefit his country as a defense.

Mr. Trump doesn't listen to me, though. Just like the *New York Times* "fake news," I am sure he sees me as nothing more than a "fake missionary." Even so, there are around a billion Catholics, I guess? I don't know exactly, though. No one knows the actual number, but anyway, Catholics make up a significant portion of the world population, so in terms of influence, the Christian church might be on par with the population of China.

So, we might not have power, but if we have authority, I would like to use some of it.

Japan is a strange country that cannot understand the religious mind

POPE'S G.S.

I was allowed to hold Mass at Tokyo Dome, but Japan is a strange country. How should I put this? It was covered in the news, but hmm... Japan is like oil that repels water. They allowed me to conduct a religious activity and there were reports on it, but the Japanese people didn't seem to understand the religious mind at all. My heart did not reach them. The only thing that reached them was the fact that Mass was held. I just don't get Japan at all.

A

We, too, would like to turn Japan into a religious country where we can talk more openly about religion and faith.

POPE'S G.S.

Hmm...

6

The Limits of His Understanding

The pope's guardian spirit laments his lack of political influence

A

There is not much time left, but I would like to ask one more question. I understand that you came to Master Ryuho Okawa today because you wanted to find out whether the messages from Jesus published in the book, *Jesus Christ's Answers to the Coronavirus Pandemic* (Tokyo: HS Press, 2020) [see Figure 1], are authentic or not. Do you have any other messages you would like to convey?

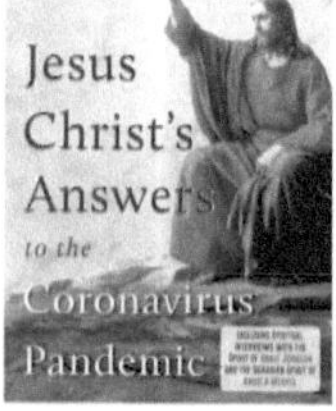

Figure 1.
Jesus Christ's Answers to the Coronavirus Pandemic

POPE'S G.S.
Umm... If Happy Science can publish spiritual messages from Jesus anywhere and anytime, then to the Vatican, it's the same as a viral infection, which will lead to the argument that the Vatican is not necessary because it shows I am not in tune with the will of Jesus.

I don't think that what I have been saying is so far off from what Christianity has traditionally been saying. I have been following the basis of Christianity that says, "We should be on the side of the weak and the poor. It is not good to occupy or attack other countries." It is true, though, that Christianity acts like this when it's weak, but changes when it gets into a position of power. But I think this is because of human nature, not its nature as a religion.

I would like to believe in your goodwill. It's just that, if Jesus appears and talks, people may criticize you by saying that Jesus is a fake and treat you like a cult. But I don't want you to face persecution again.

So, it might be a problem if you can't adjust your doctrine and teachings a little. If we could help in some way... But then, I am from the countryside in South America. I probably fail to look at things from a global perspective.

By the way, do you think my political activities are way off the mark?

A

No. A moment ago, you mentioned that you want to start by guiding those living in wealthy areas of China toward faith in Christianity. We also want to spread Happy Science teachings throughout China and make more and more people who are happy and have true faith, so in that regard, we are the same.

It's not that we hate the Chinese people. We just assert that the communist government, which suppresses and oppresses its people and tramples human rights and freedom, should be changed. In this sense, we probably feel the same as you.

POPE'S G.S.

Ah, I apologize for being so powerless. The leader of Taiwan is Christian, the chief executive of China (Hong Kong) is Christian, and the leaders of the dissident activists in China (Hong Kong) are also Christians, so I'm very sad for being so helpless in the political meaning. I'm at a loss for what to do.

"Can't Hong Kong and Taiwan try to get along with China?"

A

I'm sure it is a very difficult situation. To wrap up this interview, is there anything you would like to say to the people of Hong Kong?

POPE'S G.S.

Hmm... [*Sighs.*] I wonder if there is any way they could try to somehow build a better relationship with mainland China. I heard a rumor that the Chinese authorities are taking advantage of the situation, where people in Hong Kong cannot take to the streets because of the coronavirus, and arresting the leaders of the demonstrations. But there are Christians among those in higher positions who are arresting or issuing orders. I would like to avoid situations in which Christians are arresting other Christians. Hmm... The president of Taiwan (Tsai Ing-wen) is apparently a Christian, too. So, when I hear that Happy Science is supporting those sorts of activities in Taiwan and Hong Kong, which involve Christians, I get all confused. Maybe that is what the pope must do, but I also get the feeling that, if I were to support them, my support could accelerate China's attacks on them.

Hmm... I do not think it's good for a believer to tell people to yield to the powerful, but realistically speaking, Hong Kong and Taiwan have no hope of beating China, a superpower. So, I am wondering if they can get along with each other.

"If the spiritual messages from Jesus are real, I will retire"

B

I can clearly see that you want to prevent conflicts by showing your willingness to be on the side of the weak.

POPE'S G.S.

Well, maybe I'm not a traditional pope. I am a pope originally from one of the world's poorest countries, which is a different case from the Vatican tradition. From a Christian perspective, I could be a "revolutionary pope," but to be honest, I don't really know. Anyway, if traditional Christian ideas or what the pope is saying contradicts what Jesus is saying right now, then you can send out both messages as they are and let Christians decide which to accept.

However, if Jesus's messages you are conveying are real and he is guiding you, I will retire. There will be no need for me. I will retire because it will mean that what I am saying is incorrect. If the spiritual messages you receive are real, I will retire. I'm 83 years old, so I'll just retire. What I am doing is all contrary to what Jesus says. If Jesus does not accept what I am doing at all, I will retire.

B
Please don't say that. Jesus watches over the activities of Happy Science and strongly recommends the Christian world to awaken to their true purpose.

POPE'S G.S.
OK. Is Jesus with Hong Kong and Taiwan?

A
He is with them.

POPE'S G.S.
[*Exhales.*] So, he stands with them. That's bound to invite persecution. It is highly likely to end up like the Siege of Masada*.

Japan should also get along with China

A
That's why countries with religious faith around the world are banding together to fight materialism and atheism.

POPE'S G.S.
But you should not take the atheism of China at face value. China is an atheist nation because it wants to establish faith in Mao Zedong or faith in Xi Jinping, who hopes to be the next Mao. In fact, both politically and economically, China is rapidly Westernizing. They can't give up their wealth after having experienced it.

The coronavirus is restricting people's activities right now, but Chinese people who have made a lot of money can

* A battle in 73-74 AD, during the First Jewish-Roman War.

no longer suppress their desire to travel all over the world and enjoy themselves. Also, they understand that Mr. Abe welcomes them, so they visit a lot and spend a lot of money in Japan. Now, nearly 80 percent of Chinese people have friendly feelings toward Japan, whereas only 20 to 30 percent of Japanese people say they like Chinese people. But because Chinese people bring in a lot of money, Japan has been close with China.

So, once the virus settles, Japan will have to decide what kind of relationship they should build with the U.S. while remaining on good terms with China. My opinion is that it might be better if you could develop a relationship where you don't have to have the U.S. protect you so much.

"I don't understand why Mr. Trump is trying to protect Hong Kong and Taiwan"

POPE'S G.S.

Also, Mr. Trump passed some bills to protect Hong Kong and Taiwan, right? That doesn't make any sense to me. Why does someone like Mr. Trump, who loves crushing the strong, try to protect the weak? It doesn't make sense.

B

Faith should include justice or a cause. Of course, I agree it is good for everyone to be able to live peacefully without fighting or struggling. However, if this peaceful life means people do not have religious freedom and are only allowed to live like animals under suppression, I don't think God would tolerate it.

POPE'S G.S.

It may be just a difference in the political approach. At first, Mr. Trump seemed like a hardliner. Then, he met with North Korean leader Kim Jong-un and defended him, calling him a "friend," thereby trying to prevent a nuclear war. As a Christian, I can somewhat understand that. So, I sometimes think it may just be a difference in approach. But this kind of thing might be beyond me, a man from Buenos Aires.

A

Oh, I don't think so.

POPE'S G.S.

Ah... I don't know. It's too difficult for me to understand. I don't understand anymore. So, if Happy Science is truly correct, I will leave it to you. Hmm... I wonder, am I wrong? I don't know.

"I don't know what God is implying through the novel coronavirus infection"

POPE'S G.S.
What should we do about this virus? Many believers all around the world are praying, but I still don't know what to do. I don't understand the Will of God. I don't know why God lets so many people become infected, go through suffering, and lose their lives. Please explain. Why is it? I don't understand.

B
It could be the Divine Will; God might be telling us humans to understand something.

POPE'S G.S.
I don't understand, though. It's like a Zen riddle. Hmm...

B

I understand how you feel. But maybe now, it is necessary to look back on what you've always considered true and see if there is anything that needs to be reconsidered.

POPE'S G.S.

You, Happy Science, might not hesitate to say that the viral infection can be cured if underground Christians are officially allowed to conduct activities freely on the surface, but... [*Laughs.*]

I don't have enough confidence to go that far. I don't have the authority or the spiritual power to be able to assert that. Hmm... *The New York Times* wrote an article about Happy Science performing a rite at an empty Times Square (in New York). Does that really help wipe out the coronavirus from the city?

B

We are taught that the power of prayer increases people's immunity...

POPE'S G.S.
Actually, we have been praying a lot, too. We prayed, but a lot of people died in Italy. It hasn't improved people's immunity at all.

"I just want to know the truth"

A
I'm sorry to be rude to you, the pope, but I would like you to believe that miracles do occur. We have witnessed many miracles at Happy Science.

POPE'S G.S.
If so, Master Ryuho Okawa should come to Italy, become the next pope—the 267th pope—and communicate with Jesus. That would be much better. And, he can do that in English because Europeans understand English. If he can make miracles happen and communicate with Jesus, I want him to take my place. He's 20 years younger than me, which means he can serve for another 20 years. If what I am doing is all wrong, I have no choice but to retire. I won't ask for a retirement allowance. I don't need anything.

I just want to know the truth. I don't know the true Will of God and I don't know the will of Jesus, either. If I am guiding people in the wrong direction, please let me know. If you truly possess authority, I will obey you. Please convince me.

The Vatican has been following the precedents accumulated by the long line of popes before me and has also changed its attitude by electing someone revolutionary from South America as the pope. But if this is wrong, is the way of thinking by orthodox popes correct? I don't know.

Why on earth does Happy Science know so much about heaven anyway? I have no idea. Earlier, Master Okawa's wife (Aide to Master & CEO Shio Okawa) blocked me and said condescendingly, "After all, the pope is just a human being."

A
She didn't say it like that. She meant it respectfully.

POPE'S G.S.
[*In a slightly sarcastic way.*] Ha! I said, "I'm very sorry. With all due respect, I've come here..."

Does the difference in opinion come from the difference in views on international politics?

C
Maybe you should develop a better sense of right and wrong.

POPE'S G.S.
I can't tell! I'm not God, so I can't tell.

C
But if a divine voice comes down to you and says things that are not in line with your way of thinking, you naturally want to deny them, right?

POPE'S G.S.
Well, yeah, I don't want that to be the voice of Jesus. I wouldn't care if Buddha says things like that. Buddha can say that. If Buddha wants to make decisions and choices from his own perspective, he can say things that are different from what Jesus thinks. That's fine. But if Jesus speaks, what he says concerns us as well.

C

You have been explaining what the traditional Christian ideas are like, but for long periods of time in the past, even Christian countries approved of fighting, as you can see from the Crusades. So, it is a bit hard to tell whether your ideas are traditional or not. I think that, throughout the ages, there have probably been changes in the way of thinking developed by Christian disciples.

POPE'S G.S.

Yeah, but... I've done some studying, you know? I have been studying a little bit about what Happy Science is saying and I get the feeling that it is not only about the religious teachings. I have connections with various people around the world too, so international politics is a part of my job. And I also get the feeling that your founder and I might have different opinions on international politics. This gives me the impression that our differences don't come from the teachings, but from our opinions on international politics. I am just a man looking at the world from Buenos Aires.

Can you see the world from the perspective of God and Buddha?

C

Do you think politics is ranked above religion? It feels like you may be thinking about everything in terms of politics rather than religion.

POPE'S G.S.

Religion starts with saving the individual. You have to listen to each person's problems and save them, urge them to confess their sins, and set them on the path to God in some way. Everyone does this, but as you move up in the hierarchy, you will have to manage a greater number of people. You will have to negotiate with people more often, so your work becomes more political and your abilities are put to the test.

Some religious leaders gradually make a name for themselves as they solve people's personal problems, but after a certain point, only those who have similar qualities as company presidents and politicians are promoted higher.

C

However, the ideas that come from Master Okawa are not simply based on international politics. I believe he sees things from the standpoint of "the proper way for us to live as a human or humankind" and "what kind of mental attitude we should live with." As for the way a country should be, he sees things from the perspective of "whether the country's ways should be acknowledged as good" and "whether the people living under the country's rule are happy as children of God or Buddha." So, I would like you to understand that Master Okawa doesn't think that politics is above religion.

He is a religious leader, after all, so he interprets the world's politics from the perspective of "how things look to God or Buddha." So, I'm sorry but you might be wrong.

POPE'S G.S.

You're right. There were times when the Japanese emperor was considered a living god. I think that is what Xi Jinping is aiming to become, but this living god doesn't believe in the Spirit World, so...

C

Right.

POPE'S G.S.
In other words, it means nothing more than the most powerful worldly person.

C
I agree.

POPE'S G.S.
Right. So, I think he is wrong about that.

The pope can't become a living god even though he believes in God and the Spirit World. He will make the wrong judgments regarding worldly matters.

C
I know you, the pope, are a very prestigious person, but you and I are the same in the sense that we are both disciples. So, I can understand how you feel.

However, I think you should first accept the fact that ways of thinking beyond human comprehension sometimes come down from God and Buddha.

7

The Great Savior Surpasses the Pope

Why does Jesus come to Happy Science whose people don't pray at Saint Peter's Basilica?

POPE'S G.S.
You don't work in the kitchen, but you have conversations with your family, serve tea, and watch television together. I find this difficult to believe. Can you believe that Jesus comes and speaks to someone like that?

C
But he does.

POPE'S G.S.
How is it possible?

C
In any age...

POPE'S G.S.

I just don't understand how such a thing is possible without praying at Saint Peter's Basilica. I mean, why would Jesus come to a kitchen or a living room and speak to you?

C

I'm not really in a position to say this, but throughout the history of Christianity, there have been religious reforms many times over whether or not devotion to the church means true belief. People like Martin Luther carried out such reforms. I believe what is important is whether or not your mind is connected to God.

POPE'S G.S.

Ah, it's hard to understand. I'm really sorry for asking only the "good-hearted" people to interview me today.

A

No, please don't be.

POPE'S G.S.

If I were to lose in an argument one-sidedly, Christianity would be at great risk, so I asked for people with the nicest personalities in Happy Science. It seems like I have other visitors here today. (Two Happy Science staff members, D and E, who were scheduled to be interviewers are among the audience.) So, if any of them have anything to say, please go ahead. You can ask if you are at a distance. I'll answer your questions. This is a rare opportunity.

"I can't see what Jesus thinks since I don't have the divine supernatural powers"

D
I have a question, then.

POPE'S G.S.
OK.

D
We have strayed away from the point of argument many times, so let us get back to the beginning. The infection has spread so much in Italy, the center of Catholicism, and there seems to be a difference in the way of thinking between Jesus Christ and you.

POPE'S G.S.
Uh-huh.

D
What do you think about the difference now? Why do you think the coronavirus has spread so rampantly near the Vatican? I think that was today's main theme.

POPE'S G.S.
Could you briefly explain what Jesus said about the cause of the virus spreading?

D
He mentioned several things. I think one of the things you felt suspicious about was that Jesus himself mentioned China's biological weapons. In short, if he said so, you will lose your position. We understood that you think this way.

As C mentioned earlier, if it is the work of China, it is not in line with justice, so the U.S. will retaliate. Jesus also showed the same attitude.

Considering your current position, it sounded to me as if to say, "I can't stand this anymore. I need your help." That might have been today's main theme.

POPE'S G.S.
Ah, I see.

D
Yes.

POPE'S G.S.
If Jesus were to come down to me and I were to hear his voice in Saint Peter's Basilica, "Francis, China is researching biological weapons in Wuhan and is trying to kill hundreds of millions of people around the world," I would first suspect it to be the voice of a devil. It is totally unlikely for Jesus to say something like that.

Secondly, I don't have the divine supernatural powers, so I can't see through something like that. It's my limit.

Why are his ideas different from those of Jesus?

D
In that case, the underlying question might be, "Aren't you in a position where you must see through that Xi Jinping of China is actually a devil?"

POPE'S G.S.

Is that how you see it? It's true that Mr. Trump doesn't listen to me. Xi Jinping doesn't listen to me, either. Neither of them listens to me. They don't acknowledge my authority at all. In other words, they consider themselves superior to the pope.

This is because they possess military force. With their military might, it will be as easy as pie to stamp out Christian prayers. They will trample over the prayers of lay believers like a gigantic elephant. I think that's why they don't listen to me.

Sure, Vatican City State only has a population of just over 2,000 people, even if you include the Swiss Guard. It's the world's smallest country, so it has no worldly power. All we actually have are the power of thought and the power of faith. We are the same in this regard.

Hmm... What? That's today's main theme? "Why is what I say different from what Jesus says?" is the main theme? The only possible conclusion is, "I am not great." That's all.

It seems like God is trying to punish the U.S., too

C
Listening to you, it seems your way of looking at China and Mr. Xi Jinping is fundamentally opposite to Jesus's.

POPE'S G.S.
I am sure Xi Jinping is more important than I am.

C
He might be a devil. You used Hitler as an example a moment ago, but Shakyamuni and Jesus see Xi Jinping as the modern Hitler, or worse. Isn't it your responsibility as pope to see through it?

POPE'S G.S.
Well, looking at the fact that many more people have died in New York, it seems as if God is trying to punish the U.S., too.

C
New York is the Democratic Party's largest electoral power base in the U.S. It's an area with very strong leftist thinking.

POPE'S G.S.

Do you mean that people who didn't vote for Mr. Trump are dying, one after another? He would probably agree with that. He would accept that. He would likely just say, "You're right," because there are a lot of left-wing media outlets.

C

Many left-wingers in the area think similarly to you.

POPE'S G.S.

Yes, that's right. The starting point of western-style media is to stand up for the weak, so they tend to lean to the left. If they can learn to take a wider view of things, they can see things differently, but most journalists usually lean to the left. They write Marxist-like articles.

C

I understand you blame the U.S. for most of the misfortunes you witnessed in Argentina. However, if someone like Mr. Trump, for example, were born in Argentina and became its leader, the economy of Argentina would surely make a dramatic recovery.

POPE'S G.S.

That's an "if." People like Trump will not be born in Argentina. Souls like him choose to be born in a place where they will be able to make money, so they are not born in countries like Argentina.

Some countries in South America are experiencing an inflation rate of thousands of percent. I think top-level people in Japan can also regulate such a high inflation rate, but they are not born in South America. They choose to be born Japanese. They aren't born in places like that.

These countries are actually at a low level in politics and economy. In fact, the level of politics and economy of a country is proportional to the abilities of its people. Naturally, prayer alone doesn't solve problems.

"I do think Xi Jinping may be a devil"

POPE'S G.S.

I do think Xi Jinping may be a devil. He might be a devil, but if so, he is a pretty clever devil. He is smart only in a worldly sense, so he will be destroyed in this world. Devils are destined to ultimately lose, but up until then, they are extremely clever.

This was true of Hitler. Up until he was ruined, people thought Hitler was a savior. Germany was in tatters after WWI, but over the next 20 years, he made it one of the strongest countries in the world. Everyone at that time believed Germany was more scientifically and technologically advanced than the U.S.

That's why Japan formed an alliance with Germany and ended up being destroyed. People like him reveal themselves as devils when they are about to be destroyed, but they look like saviors until then. This is why it is sometimes difficult to tell the two apart.

"I am someone like a village chief, so I am not capable of talking about global issues"

POPE'S G.S.
Devils are quite intelligent. They are usually more intelligent than the pope. Archangels are intelligent, but so are devils. I am sure God is, of course, more intelligent than all of them. In comparison, we are no higher than village chiefs among ordinary, commonplace people. I'm probably like a chieftain. I think I am about on the level of a South

American chieftain. So, sadly, I don't think I'm capable of talking about global issues.

I was probably elected (as pope) because they (the Vatican) thought someone like me would likely understand how people in poor countries around the world feel. So, I give my opinions from that standpoint. I express my opinions from that position because it would be wrong for me to make comments from the position of the U.S. president. Few people in the world are capable of looking at things from poor people's perspectives and making comments.

[*Sighs.*] I see. So, that's the point of contention, then? All you need to do is point out, "Francis was born from the world of ordinary humans." That's the conclusion. Unfortunately, he is not a saint. That's the conclusion. If that's the case, then it's all settled.

"I did not realize that Japan has become a religiously developed country"

C

When we spoke to you before, I could keenly sense your feelings of love and gentleness. I think it is wonderful that you want to save those suffering from poverty after actually having seen them. But now, Jesus has given us his spiritual messages about the global situation from a macro perspective, so I hope you realize that his messages reflect the Voice of God spoken from a larger point of view.

POPE'S G.S.
[*Sighs.*]

C
Please open up and study his words.

POPE'S G.S.
If the Jesus that descends to you is the real Jesus, then he has obviously become smarter than the Jesus who lived 2,000 years ago. Your Jesus can't be the Jesus who worked with his disciples, the fishermen from Galilee. He can't be. Jesus was not supposed to be a person who can give opinions on international politics and the international economy. All he talked about was the human mind.

A
The time when Jesus lived and the region where he was active put limits on his teachings. Now, Jesus is in heaven, the Spirit World, and is watching over people on Earth.

He is concerned about the weak and the poor. Jesus is now sending messages through the words of Master Ryuho Okawa of Happy Science. These are spiritual facts.

POPE'S G.S.
[*Sighs.*] Well, then, the Gospel is in Japan now. If such a person has been born in Japan, that's amazing. If what you are saying is true, this may be the Advent of the Great Savior. He definitely surpasses the pope.

A
Yes, he is, but we're definitely not denying the Vatican or the Catholic Church.

POPE'S G.S.
Ah...

A
We share the desire to create a world where people with religious faith guide the Earth in a good direction, a direction in accordance with God's Will, so we sincerely hope that you will study Jesus's messages and send your message to Christians all over the world.

POPE'S G.S.
Once the coronavirus pandemic is over, please come and visit Italy again. Please be sure to come to the Vatican, too. I think it is really important that we have relations.

We, I mean Italy, are several decades behind Japan economically, but I didn't realize we were quite behind Japan religiously as well. I had no idea Japan has become such a religiously developed country, so this has been very eye-opening for me.

The pope's guardian spirit openly confesses that the Vatican's exorcisms are not effective

POPE'S G.S.
There's another man over there watching me with a serious look on his face. Please go ahead.

E
Thank you very much for today.

POPE'S G.S.
I am sorry for avoiding you several times.

E

No, it's OK, please don't be sorry. I would like to ask about an essential part of religion. My question is about miracles.

POPE'S G.S.

OK.

E

I understand there are exorcists at the Vatican.

POPE'S G.S.

Yes.

E

Happy Science will release a movie this year titled, *The Real Exorcist** in order to depict the world of actual exorcists. So, could you please tell us again how you feel about exorcists and the existence of devils, or how you feel about miracles?

* *The Real Exorcist* (Executive producer and original story by Ryuho Okawa, screenplay by Sayaka Okawa), was released in May 2020.

POPE'S G.S.
No matter what question you ask, the answer will always be the same. It will be the same.

Happy Science's exorcisms are effective, but the Vatican's exorcisms aren't. We succumb to devils most of the time. Our exorcisms hardly work. They're just the final way of consoling people. Some people who can't be cured by doctors implore us for help, so we just perform exorcisms. But we have rarely healed anyone. They might, at first, look as if they have gotten better, but once you take your eyes off of them, their illnesses come right back. You often use the expression, *joubutsu saseru* (a Japanese expression meaning, "making spirits return to heaven"). I guess we can't send devils to heaven. Anyway, we cannot expel devils to keep them from ever returning.

We can pray fervently and temporarily drive a devil out of a person's body using crucifixes, holy water, and prayers. But the devil returns to the person in less than a week, so we aren't able to treat them completely. We are not able to perform true exorcisms. Just like firefighters, all we can do is put out small fires wherever they start.

There is a very high demand for exorcisms. Every year, we get more than 500,000 requests to send exorcists, but in reality, we cannot actually respond to them all. Even if we could, we know it would be useless. When someone is actually possessed by a devil, more than 90 percent of the time, they are just sent to the hospital. In most cases, people are told to go to a mental hospital or to take medicine.

Christianity can make devils reveal their names, but can't find out the root cause of possession

POPE'S G.S.

I believe Happy Science's exorcisms really work. We conduct exorcisms as a rite, but we cannot expel devils because we cannot find out the cause of possession. We cannot determine the cause of possession and don't know what to say to the possessed people as prescriptions.

Our exorcisms can only go as far as to make the possessing devil identify itself. This is nearly identical to the principle of the mass media. Once they publish an article that brings to light some wrongdoing, that's all it takes for things to change. For example, the prime minister or cabinet ministers might be forced to resign, politicians or bureaucrats might be dismissed, and entertainers might not appear on television anymore.

It's basically no different from the mass media's principle of hindering someone's activities by bringing to light something that looks bad. The principle of our exorcisms is basically to just keep pressing until the devil reveals its name, who it truly is. Even a human being will confess something if you interrogate and torture them all day long, so it's not so difficult to get devils to say their name. Once their name is known, they are unable to remain there for some reason and they will have a harder time getting near the person. That's about as far as our exorcisms can go.

Even we don't really know how effective holy water, the Bible, and crucifixes are. Even the pope can't actually perform exorcisms. I'm sorry to say. I could perform one with a believer, but it would be nothing more than a rite.

It makes people happy, though. It makes them happy when we sprinkle holy water, touch them with crucifixes, and read the Bible. But after performing an exorcism, we can't even tell whether it worked or not. So, Happy Science is more advanced in that regard.

In the end, I guess we lose, which means Happy Science needs to grow much larger.

8
Message from the Pope's Guardian Spirit

The message he wants to convey to Christians all over the world

B
The fact that you are speaking with us today is itself a great miracle.

POPE'S G.S.
You think so? You're very kind. Thank you.

Before I came here, I was called "just a human," so I felt unsettled and found it difficult to appear. It made me upset. We had a slight argument and I asked you to create an environment where I would feel comfortable speaking. Somehow, I felt some nasty people were trying to work out a project to reveal what the Vatican is all about.

A
No, that is not our intention at all.

POPE'S G.S.

I negotiated a bit. I asked you to gather people who had graduated from Christian schools. I was told that there are not many of those, though.

Please grow much larger. In reality, you have probably already surpassed the Vatican. I would like you to work harder, so that Master Okawa becomes more influential and his messages reach the world. Although newspapers carry messages from the pope, I don't have any sort of spiritual power at all. So, I would like you to tell people about what is truly important. [*Exhales.*]

A

The pope is guiding more than a billion Catholic believers, too, so...

POPE'S G.S.

If there are, that is. If there are.

A

Catholics all over the world are seeking the salvation of Jesus through the pope. We pray that Jesus's light will also shine down on the Vatican to cure the diseases of many people, truly guiding them to heaven.

POPE'S G.S.
I understand.

Today is my second visit, right? I came once before, so we have had an exchange. (See Part Two.) This time, I came during a global pandemic. I have been suffering for a long time because I don't have power and can't do anything to help people, even though many are praying. I ended up coming here because I heard that Jesus had appeared to you.

My message to Christians all over the world is as follows. Hmm... I know there are times when people are consoled or saved by the Bible or church teachings, and it is great when people are saved this way. But if there are people who cannot be fully saved that way, they should study the teachings of Happy Science, so that they will get a better understanding of the true nature of the heavenly world and the will of Jesus.

So, in the end, the pope is only a person of this world. On the other hand, I believe Happy Science has been given some mission from the heavenly world, as if heaven lowered down a ladder. If possible, I would like to make an effort to create a complementing relationship with Happy Science, not a hating one.

From my point of view, though, I find it difficult to understand when you say, "Jesus serves as a disciple." It is difficult to accept it when I hear, "Jesus serves as the right-hand man of someone named El Cantare." Hmm, this might be because I'm just a human.

If a person like that does actually exist right now, amidst this sort of global crisis, then it's a gospel for humanity and something to be grateful for. We may just be thinking about things differently. At any rate, let's pray that the world heads in a better direction. Let's keep praying together.

B
Sure.

Words of encouragement from the pope's guardian spirit

POPE'S G.S.
Thank you very much for giving me this opportunity.

A
It's our pleasure. Thank you for speaking with us for so long.

POPE'S G.S.

Also, this wasn't scheduled, so I'm sure I caused lots of problems. I apologize from the bottom of my heart for the trouble I've caused you all as well as his wife (Shio Okawa).

Also, a little while ago, the Japanese novelist Shusaku Endo came to intervene (See Appendix) and said completely unnecessary things like, "God is supposed to be silent." This seems to be the current state of Catholicism in Japan. He has been saying things like, "God must not reply," "Jesus must not reply," and claiming that is what Catholicism is about. I feel that's a hopeless level, but that's the current state of the church. There is no reply.

C

Earlier, you mentioned that it's very unlikely for Jesus to speak in detail about the modern world. But I think the very fact that Jesus understands the modern world proves he has continued to watch over humankind from the heavenly world, even after his death. I would like you to understand that this shows God's love for humanity.

POPE'S G.S.
Sure. I would like for that to be true.

Everyone was very kind today. No one even said anything like, "The Vatican is controlled by devils." Thank you very much. I'm glad I came. I came prepared because, toward the end, I thought someone might say that. I thought someone would surely make a comment like that after I complimented Xi Jinping. Toward the end, I called on those over there (the audience) because I wanted to give them the chance to comment.

I did not mean to sound demonic. My point is just that, because many things in the world are beyond our ability, when interacting with people like him (Xi Jinping), we often need to negotiate in a worldly sense. I am sure Happy Science will face the same sort of political and diplomatic problems as you deal with other countries around the world in the future. You will probably also face economic problems. I pray that you get bigger.

I understand the HRP is now conducting political activities, but I am sure you are struggling because you are having a hard time becoming the ruling party. It is agonizing that although Hitler, as well as Mussolini, gained power, the political party with the help of the power of God cannot take political control. If a Christian organization in Japan were to form a political party, I am sure it would also be quite difficult for it to get its members elected.

It would be possible for a Christian to join an existing political party and get elected, but if they were to form a political party consisting only of Christians and undertake political activities in Japan, I doubt they would get elected. That's a difficult aspect of Japan right now, so please be tenacious and keep doing your best.

I don't know whether or not there are any Japanese archbishops and cardinals, but if someone like that were to run for office, they would not win. If a Christian were to run for office, they would not win. That is how Japan works now.

I am sure many people will have a hard time understanding you, but please keep trying. Ah, again, thank you for giving me this valuable opportunity today.

A

Thank you very much, too.

9
After the Spiritual Interview

RYUHO OKAWA
[*Claps twice.*] Ah, it's pretty hard because he argued with a completely opposite logic. The conversation went around in a circle, but I felt he somewhat gave in toward the end.

I got the impression that he was suffering from mental anguish. He is already 83, and it must be very frustrating not to be able to do anything amidst the current global crisis. All he can do is express his opinions, but even his opinions are not able to save the world. I believe he is frustrated right now. He probably came here today because his conscience led him.

Let's wrap up today's session by praying that this interview will have some sort of positive effect. [*Claps once.*] Thank you very much.

A
Thank you very much, Master Okawa.

RYUHO OKAWA
You're welcome.

CHAPTER TWO

Doubts about "Spiritual Messages from Jesus Christ"

Spiritual Interview with
the Guardian Spirit of Pope Francis

Originally recorded in Japanese on April 25, 2020,
in the Special Lecture Hall of Happy Science in Japan,
and later translated into English.

1

Background Information on the Appearance of the Pope's Guardian Spirit

The pope's guardian spirit appeared after the author reviewed the manuscript of a spiritual message from Jesus

(Translator's note: This spiritual message was recorded earlier in the morning before the session, "Spiritual Interview with the Guardian Spirit of Pope Francis" [Part One, Chapter One]. The author had finished reviewing the aforementioned *Jesus Christ's Answers to the Coronavirus Pandemic* when the pope's guardian spirit appeared in response to its contents. At the time of recording, an audio of the author's meditation ritual was playing in the background.)

C
Who are you? You look like you are in pain.

POPE FRANCIS'S GUARDIAN SPIRIT
Hah... [*About five seconds of silence.*] Hmm...

C

Who are you?

POPE'S G.S.

Hmm... Ugh... Hmm... [*Breathes heavily.*]

C

You're panting.

POPE'S G.S.

[*Breathes heavily.*]

C

Are you in pain?

POPE'S G.S.

Phew...

C

Are you in pain? Is it due to the coronavirus?

POPE'S G.S.

Phew...

C
Are you suffering from the coronavirus?

POPE'S G.S.
[*Takes a breath.*] Phew...

C
Are you Japanese?

POPE'S G.S.
[*Breathes heavily.*]

C
Are you infected by the coronavirus? (Interviewer's note: That's how much pain the spirit seemed to be in.)

POPE'S G.S.
Ah, ah, ah... Franci... Fran...

C
Huh? Xavier?

POPE'S G.S.
...cis. Francis. The pope.

C

Ah, Master reviewed the spiritual messages from Jesus today.

POPE'S G.S.

Ah. It's hard. It's painful. I'm so sad.

C

You're not currently infected with the coronavirus, are you?

POPE'S G.S.

Uh, I don't know.

C

Ah, OK. Are many people at the Vatican infected?

POPE'S G.S.

It's running rampant. We have to go outside for shopping. We can't live inside all the time. People in the Vatican, the people in the general affairs section, need to go shopping.

C

It's the same for us.

POPE'S G.S.
We need to go out on the town, in Italy.

C
You're right. Italy is in much more danger right now than Japan.

POPE'S G.S.
We can't make anything at the Vatican. It's a problem. We are praying, though.

He wants to give a message to Christians

POPE'S G.S.
I'm sorry. I understand that you have something planned with the esteemed Mr. Konosuke (Matsushita)*, but I have a message, too. Is that OK? May I give a message?

C
A spiritual message?

---

* See *Dai-Kyoukou-Jidai-o-Ikinuku-Chie Matsushita-Konosuke-no-Reigen* (literally, "The Wisdom to Survive in the Age of the Great Depression-Spiritual messages from Konosuke Matsushita-") (Tokyo: IRH Press, 2020), which was recorded on April 26, the day after the recording of this session.

POPE'S G.S.
Yes. I have a message for Christians.

C
I see. What do you want to tell them? Jesus has already given a message. He said the reason the novel coronavirus is spreading so much in Italy, where the headquarters of Christianity is located, is partly due to the Vatican's loss to China*.

POPE'S G.S.
The Vatican also needs to formally make an official statement. We need to say what we think of the coronavirus spreading throughout the world.

C
Do you know why?

POPE'S G.S.
No, I don't.

---

* On September 22, 2018, the Vatican announced that it has reached a tentative agreement with China on the issue of bishop appointment. In it, the Vatican said it will recognize the legitimacy of the seven bishops of the Chinese Catholic Patriotic Party, a church organization appointed by China.

C
Then, what message are you going to send?

POPE'S G.S.
I don't know, but I feel I need to express my feelings as a cleric. Reading the spiritual messages from Jesus caused me so much pain... It feels like the Vatican is crumbling...

C
It's because you lost to China. Also, Italy has been the main target in China's One Belt One Road Initiative.

POPE'S G.S.
I have been telling people to build bridges, not walls, but walls are being built...

C
Now, it would be better to build walls, wouldn't it?

POPE'S G.S.
There are walls everywhere.

C
Maybe you've ended up siding too much with China by saying the opposite of what Mr. Trump is doing.

POPE'S G.S.
Hmm... The book (that the author reviewed) today strongly claims that we cannot protect Christians.

C
You're right.

POPE'S G.S.
That's a bit hard on me.

C
Even if you, the pope, pray to Jesus, you might not connect with him.

POPE'S G.S.
That's why, as pope, I need to give some sort of defense or explanation.

C
A defense? Can you exorcize the coronavirus?

POPE'S G.S.
There are only around 2,000 people at the Vatican, so if we get infected, we would all die.

C
This seems to be the Divine Will, though.

POPE'S G.S.
If you claim that China did it, it can't also be the Divine Will. So, that doesn't make sense.

C
Actually, China had already been planning this. It's just that China itself also suffered some damage this time.

POPE'S G.S.
But if we just accept that as it is, there will be more wars and conflicts in the world.

Will people not believe spiritual messages from Jesus, but believe spiritual messages from the pope?

C

So, the Vatican's...

POPE'S G.S.

You're looking down on the pope, aren't you?

C

No, I'm not.

POPE'S G.S.

You think the pope is completely useless, don't you?

C

Hmm... Just a little.

POPE'S G.S.

You think I'm just an ordinary human, don't you? This is so frustrating. Oh, it's frustrating. It's upsetting.

C

I can see very well your feelings of love and gentleness, but right now, you can't fight this coronavirus without being able to properly identify justice and differentiate between good and evil.

POPE'S G.S.

I definitely don't want to be preached at by you.

C

Well, I am a religious practitioner myself. I have been taught by Jesus and Shakyamuni.

POPE'S G.S.

I don't think many people will believe the spiritual messages from Jesus, but would believe spiritual messages from the Pope.

C

People who won't believe the spiritual messages from Jesus in heaven will find it even harder to believe the spiritual messages from the pope, who is still alive. Don't you think so?

POPE'S G.S.
You know, many people refuse to believe Jesus would appear at all, whereas they can believe spiritual messages from the pope. It would seem plausible for them.

C
Even though you are still alive?

POPE'S G.S.
Yes, precisely because I am still alive.

C
Wouldn't people think it's easier for those who passed away to give spiritual messages?

POPE'S G.S.
Jesus is considered an ancient god.

C
In the sense that people don't know whether he really exists or not?

POPE'S G.S.
I don't know, but they see him as an ancient god.

C

OK, then. Can you receive the light of Jesus and channel his spiritual messages? Can we dispel the coronavirus by reading a book you wrote? Or, will doing so invite the virus?

POPE'S G.S.

Ah, I just want to pray that the souls of those who died in Italy will rest in peace.

C

I see.

POPE'S G.S.

I also want to pray for the souls of Catholics in France and Spain.

2
The Pope Recognizes Himself as a Politician More Than a Religious Leader

Will the Vatican accept the contents of the recent spiritual messages from Jesus or not?

C
Did you just come now?

POPE'S G.S.
I heard he (the author) was writing the preface and afterword for the book (*Jesus Christ's Answers to the Coronavirus Pandemic*) and realized this was going to be quite a problem...

C
Why?

POPE'S G.S.
Christianity will fall apart.

C

Ah, you mean it will fall apart if things stay as they are?

POPE'S G.S.

Since we can't do anything anymore...

C

I see. Then, we will consider recording a spiritual interview with you. (See Part One, Chapter One.)

POPE'S G.S.

But I guess it might not save people. It might just sound like an excuse.

C

No, if an excuse...

POPE'S G.S.

I can hear the voice inside your head; you think I have been reincarnating between the Realms of Desire*.

* Consists of six spiritual realms of transmigration in Buddhism, namely the hell realm, hungry spirit realm, beast realm, asura realm, human realm, and heaven realm.

C
[*Laughs.*] Between the Realms of Desire?

POPE'S G.S.
Hmm...

C
Actually, this is what I was thinking. Let's assume you gave an excuse and it spread via a spiritual interview. What if people think, "As a Christian, I should agree with the way the pope thinks" and it turns out that there is no way to stop the coronavirus from spreading? This is what I was worried about.

POPE'S G.S.
But according to that (the spiritual messages from Jesus), Jesus seems to be trying to instigate people by saying, "China is the culprit, so wage war on China."

C
Huh? Then, the Vatican...

POPE'S G.S.
We are against that.

C

You're against all war and conflict, right?

POPE'S G.S.

We can never officially admit that Jesus ever said anything like that.

C

Ah, then you're defying God.

POPE'S G.S.

I live in accordance with Jesus's teachings from 2,000 years ago.

C

In fact, Jesus is quite strict with devils.

POPE'S G.S.

If Jesus were alive now, he would not reply.

C

But he did. He replied, but...

POPE'S G.S.
We haven't heard anything.

C
Ah, that means you're not listening. Even if you had the opportunity to hear him spiritually, you would just claim, "No, those are not the teachings of Jesus." If so, you, the disciples, would be judging Jesus.

POPE'S G.S.
You're right.

C
Then, many of you will get infected by the coronavirus.

POPE'S G.S.
You claim he said something like, "This happened because China created a highly murderous weapon and dispersed it throughout the world, so attack them!" But from the point of view of Jesus's teachings, for him to say something like that is just...

If the novel coronavirus is nature's fury and not a biological weapon, it can be labeled as divine punishment

C

Then, what would the Vatican say if a biological weapon researched in Wuhan, China, were actually being used right now? How will you respond if China truly is the culprit?

POPE'S G.S.

Hmm... I would urge them to convert.

C

If it were so easy to get them to convert, the world wouldn't be suffering like this.

POPE'S G.S.

But if that were the case, it would be proving that weapon attacks based on materialism are more powerful than the belief in God.

C

The very fact that you're saying this means you don't actually believe in God. God is much greater.

POPE'S G.S.
But if it were nature's fury...

C
Yes, the pope is saying it's something like nature's fury. But this is not nature's fury.

POPE'S G.S.
If it were, then you could logically call it divine punishment. You could say, "A huge number of people are dying from this virus because they do not believe Catholicism and the pope. So, now is the time for you to convert to Christianity." However, it doesn't make much sense for so many Catholics to die.

C
Isn't it because they lack true faith and because the true teachings of Jesus have become nothing more than formalities?

POPE'S G.S.
If almost no one in Italy died, and instead, lots of people in New York and Los Angeles did, then we could issue a statement like, "This is happening because U.S. President

Trump is wrong, indeed." But lots of people died on both sides, so we can't.

C

You see! You're already assuming that. You're using the coronavirus to express what you have always thought by pointing the finger at people to say it's their fault.

POPE'S G.S.

Now, we are politicians more than we are religious leaders.

C

Unfortunately, Jesus stands with Mr. Trump, not China. Can you understand that?

POPE'S G.S.

That's strange. Because that man is more like Yahweh, the god of wrath.

C

The higher a god's level of awareness, the more clearly he reveals the differences between good and evil, or right and wrong.

Jesus was strong enough not to flee, even from crucifixion, but what about the pope?

POPE'S G.S.

I can't accept that Jesus would kill so many Italians.

C

After taking the teachings of Jesus as left-wing ideologies, they all became liberals...

POPE'S G.S.

[*Sighs.*]

C

And consider themselves to be real Christians, but in reality, Jesus is not such a strong left-winger.

POPE'S G.S.

Many poor people died in New York as well.

C

I'm sure he is going through heartache. But God also teaches that people should strive to help themselves. People actually possess much more power than they think they have, but they pity themselves and suppress it. This includes people who are not poor.

POPE'S G.S.

Christianity teaches that humans are weak.

C

Jesus is strong. If he were weak, he wouldn't have been crucified.

POPE'S G.S.

He was crucified precisely because he was weak.

C

No, no. If he truly were weak, he would have fled.

POPE'S G.S.

He was crucified because he was weak.

C

A weak person would flee the moment they face death.

POPE'S G.S.

He was crucified because he was weak.

C
If you were threatened with crucifixion, would you keep pushing forward the way you are now?

POPE'S G.S.
I would immediately resign if people said, "The coronavirus spread because Christianity has little effect, which is the pope's fault. We're going to crucify him and burn him alive."

C
Right? It would mean you're weak.

POPE'S G.S.
No, it's... Hmm... It's... That's how it would be, of course, you know?

C
What I'm saying is that Jesus was actually strong. He isn't a weak god.

POPE'S G.S.
Hmm... Well...

C
In addition, people who are deeply attached to things like worldly success and honor will immediately flee when they are about to be crucified.

POPE'S G.S.
The virus pandemic going on now is like the old Great Fire of Rome. It's to persecute Christians, I think.

C
But even Japanese people are getting infected. And so are Muslims.

POPE'S G.S.
Japan is receiving divine punishment for having so few Christians.

C
But even people in Christian countries are getting infected by the coronavirus.

POPE'S G.S.
I guess people have been "partying" too much. They don't take faith seriously.

He cannot believe that the spiritual message from Jesus is authentic

POPE'S G.S.
Ah, this isn't working. After all this talk, I guess this isn't going to save people much. OK. Sorry.

C
In fact, you might be expressing the way the majority of the world feels on behalf of them.

POPE'S G.S.
I just came in response to the spiritual messages from Jesus.

C
If we release your message together with the spiritual messages from Jesus, it might seem more plausible and authentic.

POPE'S G.S.
Please use it.

C
That might be easier for people to understand now.

POPE'S G.S.

But like you said, I have been reincarnating between the Realms of Desire... I'm just a human. I have human opinions. I am a human who makes a living through Christianity. Also, I am a politician since my organization extends throughout the world. If New York were the only place with a high death toll, I would have blamed it on Trump. But with the way things are, I can't do that. Is it rude of me to release my message after Jesus gave his spiritual messages? I don't know.

C

But even if the spiritual messages from Jesus are released, people in the world right now won't believe these very much. They will probably say, "This isn't Jesus."

POPE'S G.S.

Right. Yes. Exactly right.

C

You are clearly expressing that on behalf of them.

POPE'S G.S.

The Vatican will not believe it either, of course.

C

So, if there are people who read your opinion and think, "Ah, I felt the same way," then...

POPE'S G.S.

Some people think like you do. They think, "The pope is just a human. He's speaking as a human being who is a Christian."

C

To tell the truth, when we spoke the other day, I could tell how deep your feelings of love are (See Part Two). I respect you very much, but if there are devils in the modern world and you cannot perceive them, you must raise your level of awareness a little more.

POPE'S G.S.

Right. I agree. Your political party (the HRP) is holding a rally to mark its 11th anniversary, but why don't you forget about it and hold an official recording session with me instead?

C

We could do it as a part of our religious activities.

POPE'S G.S.

Yes.

Appendix

Spiritual Interview with Shusaku Endo

*Originally recorded in Japanese on April 25, 2020,
in the Special Lecture Hall of Happy Science in Japan,
and later translated into English.*

Shusaku Endo (1923 - 1996)

Japanese author. Baptized as Catholic at the age of 12. He won the Akutagawa Prize for *Shiroi Hito* (literally, "White Men"). At the age of 38, he had three operations for pulmonary tuberculosis and struggled against the disease for two years. Major works include *Chinmoku* (literally, "Silence"), *Kirisuto no Tanjo* (literally, "The Birth of Christ"), and *Fukai Kawa* (literally, "Deep River").

The unexpected appearance of the spirit of Shusaku Endo

(Translator's note: This spiritual interview was recorded when the spirit of Shusaku Endo, a deceased Japanese author, came to express his opinion just when the recording of the spiritual interview with the guardian spirit of the pope [included in Part One, Chapter One of this book] was about to take place. This delayed the scheduled recording of the spiritual interview with the guardian spirit of the pope for 30 minutes. During this session, the audio of Master Ryuho Okawa's meditation ritual was playing in the background.)

RYUHO OKAWA
Why? ...why this being? How strange.

C
I'm sorry?

RYUHO OKAWA
This being shouldn't be here. He identifies himself as Shusaku Endo, but he is not supposed to be here... It could be because he was a Catholic?

C

Wait. Mr. Shusaku Endo already passed away.

RYUHO OKAWA

He was a Catholic. The author of *Silence*, Mr. Shusaku Endo.

C

Ah, is this because I mentioned him the other day?

RYUHO OKAWA

Did you?

C

I said in a book*, "I have a feeling that the religious persecution portrayed in *Silence* might become a reality."

RYUHO OKAWA

Shusaku Endo... A Catholic.

C

What did he come here for?

---

* See *Chugoku-Hatsu-Shingata-Coronavirus Jinrui-e-no-Kyokun-wa-Nani-ka* (literally, "The Novel Coronavirus Originated in China: Lessons for Humankind-Spiritual messages from Shibasaburo Kitasato and R. A. Goal-") (Tokyo: IRH Press, 2020). Its English translation is scheduled to be published this summer.

RYUHO OKAWA
I don't know. Maybe he is here as the pope's messenger [*laughs*].

C
But why Mr. Shusaku Endo?

RYUHO OKAWA
This has something to do with Catholicism. Why did you come here...?

"Silence" is correct, so God must not speak?

SHUSAKU ENDO
I have something to say.

C
No, we don't need you. Why did you come? Or did you come only to be here?

SHUSAKU ENDO
You know, God must keep silent.

F
He will not keep silent.

C
God is never silent. It's just that you couldn't hear Him because your mind was distorted.

SHUSAKU ENDO
I was president of The Japan P.E.N. Club.

C
What kind of connection has brought you here today?

SHUSAKU ENDO
When Happy Science protested against the content of an article in *Friday* magazine, I argued that what you were doing was wrong. I said that freedom of speech should be protected, but God does not have freedom of speech. God must be silent.

C
The coronavirus is now spreading because there are so many people without faith and who have become arrogant enough to believe they are above God, just like you.

SHUSAKU ENDO
The important thing is whether you abandon your faith or not.

C
So, you mean you are in hell now?

SHUSAKU ENDO
I don't know.

C
You are in hell, right?

SHUSAKU ENDO
How would I know that?

C
I'm sure you are in hell.

SHUSAKU ENDO
My state of mind is the same as the pope, so how would I know? God doesn't answer my prayers even when I pray.

C

God does answer.

SHUSAKU ENDO

Like I said He doesn't.

C

Please listen to me properly.

SHUSAKU ENDO

Like I wrote in the book, *Silence*, there are no answers.

C

Let me tear your "Silence" into pieces.

SHUSAKU ENDO

Keeping silent is correct. God must not speak.

C

Do you think you are God?

SHUSAKU ENDO

God is, like I said, silent.

C
Then, why does God exist?

SHUSAKU ENDO
God doesn't exist.

C
Yes, He does!

SHUSAKU ENDO
He doesn't exist in the human world.

C
If He is not in the human world, how did the Bible or the Koran come into existence?

SHUSAKU ENDO
God doesn't answer. So, those scriptures are all fake. God is God because He doesn't answer.

C
If so, all religions would be fake.

SHUSAKU ENDO
Yeah, human beings created them.

C
Don't be overtaken by pseudo-religion.

God is a fictional figure that novelists in the past created

SHUSAKU ENDO
God is the product of imagination.

C
[*Smiles wryly.*]

SHUSAKU ENDO
That is why authors can be authors. God is a fictional figure. So, it is wrong to say God really exists. He is a fictional figure.

C

We, Happy Science, are publishing books urgently* amid the spread of the coronavirus. In other words, this is a spiritual battle about whether God really exists or not.

SHUSAKU ENDO

You should know that there are even Christians like me who don't believe in God. God has served for nothing. At the time of the plague epidemic or the Spanish flu epidemic, God just left people to die. He neglects us and leaves us all to die.

C

Such plagues spread and cull people out because people like you are disseminating such thoughts and corrupting human beings, am I right?

SHUSAKU ENDO

I was even awarded an honor medal from the Vatican.

---

* Happy Science urgently published the book titled, *Jesus Christ's Answers to the Coronavirus Pandemic* (Tokyo: HS Press, 2020).

C

Why do you believe in the Vatican? You believe there is no such thing as a religion, don't you?

SHUSAKU ENDO

I believe in what humans created, not what God created.

C

Don't you think that is a foolish idea? Did you receive such an honorary medal out of the desire for fame?

SHUSAKU ENDO

I am saying that God is a fictional figure, something that novelists in the past created.

C

If you think that religions are fiction, you should not have received the award from the Vatican.

SHUSAKU ENDO

We are all the same human beings, so there's no problem.

C

You make me sick.

SHUSAKU ENDO

There is a hierarchical relationship between humans.

C

Please leave.

SHUSAKU ENDO

I can't stand up. I have to be silent.

C

You don't have any authority.

SHUSAKU ENDO

He is already in a coffin.

C

If you say so, I will summon (the Archangel) Gabriel*.

SHUSAKU ENDO

God is already in a coffin.

---

* One of the most famous of the so-called Seven Archangels. In Judaism, Christianity, and Islam, Gabriel is said to be a messenger of God, and even today, Gabriel is believed to be the guardian of communication. See *Dai-Tenshi-Gabriel-no-Reigen* (literally, "Spiritual Message from Archangel Gabriel") (Tokyo: Happy Science, 2014), only available in Japanese, which was recorded on June 26, 2014.

C
Gabriel [*claps twice*].

SHUSAKU ENDO
God can't.

C
Gabriel [*claps twice*].

SHUSAKU ENDO
He must never speak a word.

C
Gabriel [*claps three times*].

SHUSAKU ENDO
There's no point in calling Gabriel.

C
Archangel Gabriel [*claps four times*].

SHUSAKU ENDO
It is said that Gabriel delivered messages from Allah, but it will soon become clear if it was a lie or not.

C

No, it is not a lie. He has already given us some spiritual messages and said that he has a connection with Islam.

SHUSAKU ENDO

No, it must be a lie. It's a fiction.

C

[*Smiles wryly.*]

SHUSAKU ENDO

Well, Islam itself is a fiction, so that is why it taught that Allah does not directly deliver messages to human beings. Gabriel served as a messenger on Allah's behalf.

PART TWO

Finding His Character and True Thoughts

Spiritual Interview with the Guardian Spirit of Pope Francis

Originally recorded in Japanese on January 14, 2020, in the Special Lecture Hall of Happy Science in Japan, and later translated into English.

1

Thoughts on Nuclear Weapons and Faith

The guardian spirit of Pope Francis appears

(Translator's Note: This spiritual interview was recorded on January 14 before the novel coronavirus spread worldwide. A large number of people were found to be infected in Wuhan, China, but there were none in Italy. Also, there were tensions between the U.S. and Iran due to the killing of General Soleimani by the U.S. 10 days before this recording. Further, the pope visited Japan last year in November 2019 for the first time in 38 years.

This recording took place after the author finished watching the movie, *The Two Popes* [released on Netflix in 2019], when the guardian spirit of Pope Francis visited him. During the recording, the audio of Happy Science's sutra, "The True Words Spoken By Buddha" was playing in the background.)

C

Is someone there?

POPE'S GUARDIAN SPIRIT
Pa, pa, papa. Papa, papa, papa, papa. Papa. Papa. Papa.

C
Papa? Not the pope?

POPE'S G.S.
Papa.

C
Are you Papa?

POPE'S G.S.
Yes. I am papa.

C
Are you the pope?

POPE'S G.S.
Yes.

C
Good evening. Are you the current pope?

POPE'S G.S.
Yes.

C
Mr. Bergoglio?

POPE'S G.S.
Francis.

C
Pope Francis?

POPE'S G.S.
Papa. Ah...

[*About five seconds of silence.*] Franc... Francis...

C
Francis-co?

POPE'S G.S.
Yes [*exhales*].

C
From Argentina?

POPE'S G.S.

Yeah.

C

When we spoke in the afternoon, you said you could speak a little bit of easy Japanese...

POPE'S G.S.

Ah.

C

Is that right?

POPE'S G.S.

My Japanese isn't very different from my English speaking.

C

I see.

POPE'S G.S.

I speak it brokenly.

C

I see. I'm sorry that I cannot speak Spanish.

POPE'S G.S.
It's OK.

Impressions of the film, *The Two Popes*

POPE'S G.S.
[*About five seconds of silence.*] Ah, you were watching the movie.

C
Yes, we were watching *The Two Popes*, and that's when you (spiritually) appeared.

POPE'S G.S.
Yeah. That's right. It was nominated for the Academy Awards.

C
Yes, the actors like Anthony Hopkins have been nominated.

POPE'S G.S.
That's not a very good thing.

C
Is that so?

POPE'S G.S.
It's not very good to make a movie about the scandals and cover-ups of popes.

C
You're right. Those issues really shouldn't become the subject of movies.

POPE'S G.S.
No, they shouldn't. They shouldn't be publicized. They shouldn't be shown as if they saw what really happened. They must not depict things that have not happened as if they had.

Impressions of Japan and an appeal for the abolition of nuclear weapons

C
You recently came to Japan, right?

POPE'S G.S.
Yes, I did.

C
What did you think?

POPE'S G.S.
Nagasaki...

C
Yes.

POPE'S G.S.
Hiroshima...

C
Yes.

POPE'S G.S.
Tokyo...

C
Yes.

POPE'S G.S.
Ah... I was very sad.

C
You were sad?

POPE'S G.S.
Yes.

C
About the atomic bombs?

POPE'S G.S.
Hmm... Nagasaki and Hiroshima... So sad... [*Sighs*]. Japan must take the initiative and create a nuclear-weapon-free nation. It must get other countries to do the same.

America is scattering its nuclear weapons around the world. That's not good. Many Japanese people died from atomic bombs. You have the right to say, "We do not need America's atomic or hydrogen weapons."

C
Can you not as the pope say this in the United States or China?

POPE'S G.S.
Just because you have these weapons does not mean you are protected. In fact, you may get targeted just for having them.

C
Right.

POPE'S G.S.
North Korea is a good example of that. They think that they are protecting themselves by having nuclear weapons. But they cannot complain if they are attacked precisely because they possess them.

C
What about Iran? They were attacked even though they haven't yet developed nuclear weapons.

POPE'S G.S.
If they really wanted to, they could get their hands on Russian-made nukes. So, it isn't impossible for them to fight.

Will Japan, which hosts U.S. military bases, be attacked by North Korea or China?

POPE'S G.S.
In the end, it's about whether it is right or not. Even we at the Vatican do not use nuclear weapons to defend ourselves. We would be wiped out if one were dropped on us. We are such a small city. All it would take is one bomb. But we are working hard to make sure there is no just reason to do that. How Japan should defend itself is a difficult issue. Hmm... I am afraid that America's role as a deterrent will push Japan back into war.

C
America's role as a deterrent?

POPE'S G.S.
Yes. Japan thinks the U.S. will protect them. But Japan hosts U.S. bases and the U.S. possesses nuclear weapons. So, Japan is at risk of attack from North Korea, China, and Russia.

C

Well, according to the way China's Xi Jinping currently thinks, he apparently plans for Japan to be off the map by 2050 (because it will be a part of China).

POPE'S G.S.

Hmm...

C

He has plans that give the impression that his true intention is to invade Japan.

POPE'S G.S.

You should show them that China doesn't exist on the map.

C

[*Smiles wryly.*] That will only start a conflict.

POPE'S G.S.

Yeah? Make it look like their country was taken by India.

If Xi Jinping is going to massacre everyone, then people should abandon their faith

C

Many Christians are being oppressed in China, but what are your thoughts about it?

POPE'S G.S.

It is miserable. We have no military. But we wouldn't be able to help them even if we had one.

C

How do you see Hong Kong?

POPE'S G.S.

Hong Kong is miserable.

C

Now, there are demonstrators that are singing hymns as they protest.

POPE'S G.S.

Yes, in the modern age, we cannot stop missiles by calling out God's name.

C

How should Hong Kong be toward China?

POPE'S G.S.

China will probably tell the people not to have religious faith.

C

Yes.

POPE'S G.S.

Faith helps people to unite.

C

It's also because China is very materialistic.

POPE'S G.S.

Aside from Christians, there are Buddhists, Taoists, and others (in Hong Kong). There are only about a million Christians. They do not make up all seven million. If the people are going to be massacred by Xi Jinping as the Jews were by the Nazis in the Holocaust, then I think they should abandon their faith.

C
Really?

POPE'S G.S.
Yes.

C
Oh.

POPE'S G.S.
Yes, because God would be meaningless to you, if you lose your life.

C
Are you saying that God's true blessing in this world is to protect our lives?

POPE'S G.S.
I don't believe that it is God's wish for all seven million people in Hong Kong to be killed and...

C
No, I don't think God wishes for that either.

POPE'S G.S.
I do not think that God wishes for nuclear missiles to be dropped on mainland China and for many to be killed to protect Hong Kong from getting occupied, either.

C
Do you mean that when a country with expansionist ambitions appears, the world should just submit to them?

POPE'S G.S.
That has happened many times in history. The Jesuits even traveled with the military to the other side of the globe to spread God's word.

2

Ideas Derived from the Experience of Surviving under a Military Regime

Surviving under the Argentine military dictatorship and later becoming a pope

C

I understand that Argentina was ruled by a military dictatorship for some time.

POPE'S G.S.

That's right. Yes.

C

I think that the people at the time were suffering under an oppressive regime.

POPE'S G.S.

Oh, it was terrible.

C

Even if they manage to preserve their life...

POPE'S G.S.

Priests and nuns were killed too.

C

Yes.

POPE'S G.S.

I was accused of having made compromises. I do not know if it was consistent with God's Will for me to survive and become a pope.

C

I think that truly innocent people were killed during that time. But do you think it is better to stay alive even if it means becoming a part of such an oppressive system with such a philosophy?

POPE'S G.S.

A faith that cannot save its people is pitiful. In the end, the U.K. went to war against Argentina... Militaries are never good at economics.

C

That military regime (in Argentina) appears to have collapsed during Thatcher's time...

POPE'S G.S.

Hmm... There are a number of other military regimes in different countries that I wish would collapse. Like the one in Thailand, for example.

C

They have a military-run government.

POPE'S G.S.

Even a country like that has one.

Stating reconciliation with Iran as "difficult" and referring to Iran's religious affairs

POPE'S G.S.

But I think the world is most concerned* with Iran.

---

* At the time of the recording of this spiritual interview (January 14, 2020), the U.S.-Iran relation was becoming tense as Iran launched ballistic missiles as a retaliatory attack in response to Iranian General Soleimani having been killed in an air strike by an American drone.

C

Yes. I think even the Iranian problem is somewhat a conflict between a Christian nation and an Islamic nation.

POPE'S G.S.

Yes.

C

How do you view this as a pope?

POPE'S G.S.

Well, to give you my honest impression as a single human being, I do not approve of Trump because he is extremely self-righteous. But I think it is very difficult to make peace with Iran.

C

Hmm...

POPE'S G.S.

I don't think they will listen.

C

But we should at least try to talk...

POPE'S G.S.
Hmm... That may not be possible.

C
Do you mean it'll be difficult?

POPE'S G.S.
Right. If they acquire nuclear weapons, they will most likely destroy the Vatican as well. That's the kind of country they are.

C
Well, in the same way that you are speaking to us in spiritual form, we are able to hear what Trump's guardian spirit and the guardian spirits of Iran's supreme leader and the president have to say.

POPE'S G.S.
Yes, it's impressive. Amazing.

C
From what I've personally heard, according to their subconscious thoughts, Christians, like Mr. Trump, are the ones that equate Islam with evil.* That is the impression I get.

POPE'S G.S.
Yes, you're right. They are quite arrogant.

C
The Muslims have said their religion has always accepted Christianity and Judaism from the very beginning, and that they do not believe these faiths are evil.

POPE'S G.S.
They don't acknowledge them now.

C
I see.

POPE'S G.S.
We cannot spread Christianity in Iran now.

* See Ryuho Okawa, *U.S.-Iran Conflict: The Spiritual Reason and Way to Peace – Spiritual Messages from the Spirit of General Soleimani and the Guardian Spirits of President Trump and President Rouhani* – (Tokyo: HS Press, 2020).

C

Maybe not Christianity...

POPE'S G.S.

Neither can Buddhism be spread there. Convert and it would mean death.

C

Isn't it possible for Christians and Muslims to accept each other?

POPE'S G.S.

Muslims can, say, leave Iran and go to the U.S. or Europe and convert to another religion. But if they did that in Iran, they would most likely get killed.

C

But I saw a CNN correspondent reporting from Iran from within a group of emotional people who were vocally mourning during Soleimani's funeral.

POPE'S G.S.

That correspondent was not Iranian.

C
You mean it would not have been safe for a Christian Iranian?

POPE'S G.S.
That person was there just as a reporter.

C
I see.

His answers in terms of right and wrong regarding the whole issue

POPE'S G.S.
Hmm... [*About five seconds of silence.*] You Japanese people claim to be non-religious, so you have no belief, but you also have a system that accepts all faiths. So, your country seems extremely simple yet confusing at the same time. I had thought Japan would be a good platform to deliver my message from.

I have seen a military dictatorship. I never again want to see a military occupation, oppression, or massacre. There are occasions when the military can come in useful, but 90 percent of the time, militaries do bad things. The most you need is the police force. That would be enough. You don't need anything more than that.

C

But it was a Christian country that dropped the atomic bomb on Japan.

POPE'S G.S.

Hmm.

C

In terms of this, what do you...

POPE'S G.S.

That is a difficult issue, so I cannot say anything about it. Christian nations, including Catholics... [*sighs*], traveled the world, creating colonies all throughout Asia and Africa. While I am the pope, I do not have the authority to give a righteous statement on this issue. I am not in a position to be able to make judgments on the thoughts and decisions of the popes and kings of the past several hundreds of years. It's not that I can. But looking back from our perspective today, it certainly appears like an incredible act of aggression.

In Nagasaki, Japan, where an atomic bomb was dropped, Christianity had been spreading but a lot of Christians were killed, weren't they? They were persecuted because they were not in line with Japan's fundamental structure.

Tens of thousands or hundreds of thousands of Christians were killed. These types of mistakes... You see, Japan was a samurai nation, so it fought off Western infiltration at the shoreline. But some countries that were not strong enough to do that were conquered completely, like Peru and the rest of South America. Well, I do not have the wisdom, authority, power, or level of awareness to be able to talk about right and wrong in relation to the entire situation. I am sorry, but I am just a human being.

C
Don't worry.

"I want the U.S. to accept refugees"

C
The word "wall" was mentioned a lot in the movie, too. Considering that it was made recently, I felt that maybe

they were using the word as a way of protesting against Trump's wall.

POPE'S G.S.
People want to escape from countries that have been taken over by a military regime. So, we must give them the freedom to escape. A wall will prevent them from doing that, so... [*Sighs.*]

C
So, are you saying that there are people who cannot escape unless they come in as illegal immigrants?

POPE'S G.S.
Trump won't allow such immigrants. These people have nowhere to go. The people of Egypt or Central and South America who need help have nowhere to go. Most people in South America do not like the U.S.

C
But the illegal immigrants coming in from Mexico are not just people seeking refuge. Some are a part of drug cartels. Some Americans living on the border have been killed by them.

POPE'S G.S.

These countries are poor. The problem is that they are poor. No one would leave if their nation were prosperous. A lot of refugees have also been crossing the Mediterranean from Syria and Turkey or even deeper inland. That is because their countries are terrible, isn't it?

C

Hmm...

POPE'S G.S.

I can understand why refugees are not welcome. It is because it will disturb the peace and order in the host country. But these refugees would get killed if they remained in their home country. So, the concern is that refugees will bring down living standards. But countries that have a lot of food—bread, milk, and juice—must accept at least some of these people. If every country were to adopt their own version of "America First," it would not be good.

Relationship with St. Francis of Assisi and Jesus Christ

C

You have been very passionate about eradicating poverty since the time you were in Argentina.

POPE'S G.S.

Yes, I have.

C

I am sure you must be a modest and very approachable man. I heard that you took your name, "Francis," from St. Francis of Assisi, so the poor will not be forgotten.

POPE'S G.S.

Yes, that's right.

C

Have you met St. Francis of Assisi?

POPE'S G.S.

No, he is a much greater man than I.

C

I see.

POPE'S G.S.

Modern popes may have more worldly authority. But not Francis... Instead, he had spiritual power. He had spiritual authority.

C

So, do you respect St. Francis of Assisi?

POPE'S G.S.

He is much, much closer to Jesus Christ.

C

I see. When you came here in the evening, I asked, "Are you able to meet with Jesus Christ?" You answered, "He is far away."

POPE'S G.S.

No, no, no, no, no. That would be impossible. He is much, much greater. It's like Dubai's...

C
Tallest building?

POPE'S G.S.
It's just like how someone living in a house made of mud cannot meet someone living at the very top of a building like the one in Dubai that is more than 800 meters tall.

C
I see, that is how large you see the distance between yourself and Jesus Christ.

POPE'S G.S.
I am no different from a human being living on the earth.

C
But from listening to you, I can tell that you are very humble and without conceit or arrogance, even after becoming pope.

POPE'S G.S.
No, I am not. I am weak. I am a weak human who is very fearful. So many of the people I knew were caught and killed. They prayed to God and repented but no one was

saved. They were all killed. I was unable to be a shield and protect them. All I could do was to befriend the commanders of the military and try to appease them. I was the only one that survived, and those who were true to their beliefs and resisted, even clergies, were all killed. So, I am powerless, just powerless, powerless, powerless... Even the Roman Catholic pope is powerless. Powerless against Beijing. Powerless against the U.S. I spoke in Japan, but it felt like I was beating the air. My voice disappeared into the mountains. It didn't echo. Christians in Japan are weak. They have no political power. None at all.

Hope for a peaceful world without war and aversion to conflict

C

But, in some sense, Hongkongers can exert their power. It would still be meaningful for you to speak in Hong Kong.

POPE'S G.S.

Well, the people of Hong Kong are prosperous. In the end, they will be able to escape abroad. They have not come to the point where the military administration has been established as it was in Argentina. They are fighting to regain their freedom. There is still restraint as China is, deep down, not eager to lose Hong Kong's prosperity and affluence. Hong Kong makes the most money from trade with foreign countries. That is why they are refraining from shooting missiles at it so easily. They know that if they destroy those skyscrapers, all they would have are ruins. So, it's up to what China decides to do.

Taiwan won in its election,* so Taiwan and Hong Kong will probably become very close. They will also try to form relationships with the U.S., U.K., and Japan in order to survive.

C
I see that your experience of having been in a country where you would have been immediately killed if you had raised your voice is influencing your views and philosophy.

POPE'S G.S.
That is why I feel so sorry for countries like Iraq, Iran, and Syria. They are unable to do anything and it is the citizens that suffer because of their civil war. They are not sure

* Three days before the recording of this spiritual interview, on January 11, 2020, in Taiwan's presidential election, Tsai Ing-wen, who opposes China, was re-elected with a record number of votes.

what is right anymore. I guess all they want is order and stability. Because they can't have jobs during a war. So, I think a peaceful world without war is good. I don't think that simply opposing such forces is always the best idea.

"They don't need to walk right into their own Holocaust"

POPE'S G.S.

A moment ago, I said a very shameful thing as a pope. I said, "If the people in Hong Kong are going to be killed (by China), then they should abandon Christianity, Buddhism, or Taoism." But they can still believe in their hearts. It would be impossible to fight against a tank just by expressing these beliefs in some form. Yeah, I have seen many dead bodies, so I've had enough.

C

In the case of Hong Kong, if they don't take action now, then they will be integrated into China and—worst-case scenario—the area could become like what Argentina experienced.

Do you mean that, even if people ultimately end up living under an authoritarian regime as you had in Argentina, you still think it would be better for them not to take action, so that they can live?

POPE'S G.S.
I'm worried that, if they start throwing petrol bombs, tanks will soon enter. We have many official churches and underground churches in mainland China. There are said to be 100 million believers, but we have no way of knowing for sure. The right to appoint priests belongs to Rome, or rather to the Vatican, but Xi Jinping says, "Give that right to me. If you give it to me, their (the citizens) safety is ensured. If you don't, I'll kill them." In such a case, I'm weak. I'll end up saying, "If you're going to be killed, then you would rather switch sides." I'm sorry for being this way.

C
Well, but maybe, sometimes, even gods might say the same thing. The time will come when you must try again.

POPE'S G.S.
[*Exhales.*] Well...

C

But I believe it is best to have faith in your heart.

POPE'S G.S.

Yeah, because Xi Jinping will die someday. So, this won't last forever. Someone else may take over. But I don't think they need to walk right into their own Holocaust. The reason the U.S. went so far as to drop an atomic bomb on Japan was that Japan was strong and resisted, right? That is why Japan launched surprise attacks on Hawaii in the U.S., right?

So, when the Islamic terrorists destroyed the One World and Two World Center, they were probably imitating Japan. They started a war even though they didn't have the capacity to win. That is why the whole country was devastated and several hundreds of thousands died. So, terrorist leaders also have to be careful because they have a responsibility not only to themselves but to others as well.

"I did a good job of surviving without giving the enemy any excuses"

C

When you were in Argentina while it was under a military dictatorship, you did the best you could while maintaining your faith in your heart. Then, Argentina's military dictatorship collapsed due to influence from the U.K., an outside country. You've been making comments like that because you have experience surviving through this method, right?

POPE'S G.S.

Yes. If we are too hardline, we will be playing into the opposition's expectations and also be giving them an excuse. We have to be wise about it. Japanese Christians were killed by Japanese feudal warlords in the past, as well as by Americans. It is ironic that they dropped an atomic bomb on Nagasaki.

C

That's true. Nagasaki had the largest number of Christians in Japan...

POPE'S G.S.

Right? Maybe Okinawa might be the next target because they host U.S. military bases. Will they be attacked or protected because of the bases? I'm sure the anxiety makes it hard for residents to sleep.

3
Strong Desire to Save the Vulnerable

"I feel that I should always be on the side of the vulnerable"

C
Judging from the state of modern China, I believe they would want to take advantage of this situation and invade regardless of whether or not there are any U.S. military bases. Since they are planning on taking control of certain areas, especially Okinawa, as their territory anyway, it would actually be more dangerous not to have U.S. military bases.

POPE'S G.S.
Well, Japan has won before and only lost once. It has won many more times than that. So, you may be able to prepare well enough. If Kyushu and Okinawa are strong, then Taiwan and Hong Kong may not be taken. I don't know exactly, because I'm not a politician. But... how should I put it... I hope that a revolution for peace happens in China.

C

Yes. More of the world needs to be able to accept religious faith.

POPE'S G.S.

Well, I don't like materialism either. But as for me, who sits at the foot of the table of Jesus's disciples, I think I should support the weak. The strong already have many people on their side. They can solve things by themselves. So, I feel that I should always be on the side of the vulnerable. I cannot help but think about how to save, protect, or liberate those who are being persecuted or oppressed.

"America's criteria at judging the right and wrong is extremely vague"

C

On the other hand, Iranians are now going beyond seeing things in terms of loss and gain... Looking at Trump's present way of negotiating, as Master says, since people are motivated by loss and gain, Trump negotiates like a businessman.

POPE'S G.S.

Seems like that's working a bit.

C

Yes, it is somewhat working for China and North Korea.

POPE'S G.S.

In order to create a reason to invade militarily, Trump imposes economic sanctions on his own, making life for the Iranian people difficult. This will incite a riot against the Iranian government and then Trump will take advantage of these disturbances to invade militarily under the pretense of helping the people. It's the age-old story of how countries are stolen.

C

Hmm... That's not really very fair...

POPE'S G.S.

It doesn't make me feel good.

C

Me either.

POPE'S G.S.
If a dictatorship is just killing people for no reason, it should be destroyed. Governments like Pol Pot must be destroyed.

C
I agree.

POPE'S G.S.
The U.S. sanctions are making the country struggle and the people are getting out of control. The U.S. took advantage of this and said, "I killed the commander to free you. I will shoot a lot of missiles and defeat the military government of your country." The criteria for judging good and evil are extremely vague here.

C
America is said to be making use of various forms of those types of manipulative strategies.

POPE'S G.S.
The U.S. is building a wall against Mexico. And against Iran, they are going to invade with their military, right?

C

Hmm...

POPE'S G.S.

So, I have doubts about this way of thinking.

"Successful Christian countries must not occupy or attack other countries out of arrogance over their success"

C

Iranian people[*] too have said that there is no justice in such way of thinking, but that they also don't want to abandon

[*] This refers to the spirit of Ayatollah Khomeini, the guardian spirit of Ayatollah Khamenei, the guardian spirit of President Rouhani, and the spirit of General Soleimani. See Ryuho Okawa, *Spiritual Messages from the Guardian Spirit of Ayatollah Khamenei and General Soleimani - For the Mutual Understanding between Iran and the U.S. –* (Tokyo: HS Press, 2020) and aforementioned *U.S.-Iran Conflict: The Spiritual Reason and Way to Peace – Spiritual Messages from the Spirit of General Soleimani and the Guardian Spirits of President Trump and President Rouhani –*.

the ethnic and religious culture of their country or their pride.

POPE'S G.S.
There are over a billion Muslims in the world. To Mr. Trump, this is a mystery. So, for Iranian people, it's hard to understand why the U.S. wants to conquer the Muslim world just to protect Israel, which only has nine million people. America says, "It's because they're behind the times," but there are many other countries like that...

C
Yes, they are.

POPE'S G.S.
There are. It can't be helped. Because they haven't had industrial revolutions yet. They claim that these countries are behind Europe, but that's natural because Europe is wealthy. And that's exactly why they have an obligation to save them. Well... this issue is difficult for me, so I am not exactly sure, though. Sending out a message of peace is all I can do. I cannot see Jesus even when I pray hard. Where is he off to?

C

From what you've been saying, I feel your love toward vulnerable and oppressed people in countries around the world. So, I am grateful that you have those feelings as a pope.

POPE'S G.S.

I think Islam is also trying to treat poor people equally. You can see it spreading in poor countries like Africa.

C

Yes.

POPE'S G.S.

China's Communism was originally on the side of the weak, but in reality, they are working in a different direction, right? That's why I think we, Christian people, need to have the way of thinking that we are on the side of the weak. Many Christian nations are successful, but they shouldn't occupy and attack other countries out of arrogance over their success.

4

Complex Feelings toward China

Jesus's branch souls that fought against totalitarianism and communism

C

Jesus also spoke* at the end of last year, saying that the pope must now surely be in deep agony. He also told us, "Superiority or inferiority of religion cannot be judged by the superiority or inferiority of civilization, science, or military might. I don't want people to fight thinking that winning would prove the victor's religion to be superior."

POPE'S G.S.

Jesus's strengths were not in politics and economics. I don't think he understands much about those sorts of things. They weren't mentioned in the Bible either.

C

However, in Happy Science, since Master has great spiritual power, we are able to hear from, for example, John

* See "Spiritual Messages from Jesus Christ" recorded on December 7, 2019. This video can be watched at Happy Science local branches and temples worldwide.

Lennon... from the Beatles, who appeared a little in the movie we watched.

POPE'S G.S.

Yes, yes.

C

It has recently been discovered that John Lennon and Tolstoy* are figures as which parts of Jesus's soul worked.

POPE'S G.S.

Oh, really?

C

John Lennon clearly criticized Mao Zedong in the song called "Revolution." And in part of the song "Power to the

* See Ryuho Okawa, *John Lennon's Message from Heaven* (Tokyo: HS Press, 2020) and "Tolstoy – Jinsei ni Okuru Kotoba" (lit. "Tolstoy – Gift of words for your life") recorded on August 24, 2012.

People," he incorporated his desire to fight against such totalitarian regimes and he did activities based on this desire also.

POPE'S G.S.
Yeah, but communism has lasted for 70 years.

C
Hmm...

POPE'S G.S.
Communism hasn't been defeated yet, right? It's not easy.

"I do not like China, but also do not hope for nuclear war between the U.S. and China"

C
Communism now only survives by concealing itself under the economy, so...

POPE'S G.S.

If a country is really bad, it would start to break down internally. But China has a good outward disguise, so it's difficult to know the truth. I don't even like China that much. They are repressing religions and underground churches, taking people's freedom of belief and thought, and even trying to steal papal authority. Their ambitions are so apparent. I think some strong country needs to stand in their way.

C

Ultimately, Xi Jinping just wants to be a god too. But, right now...

POPE'S G.S.

But as a pope, I can't say that I hope for nuclear war between the U.S. and China.

C

I understand.

POPE'S G.S.

I don't want to encourage anything that would cause hundreds of millions of people to die. I hope for peace.

"I think we need people who can express their opinions to China sternly"

C

But when we look at how China is currently treating Christianity, the government seems like it's struggling to put religion under its political influence and bind God under the law.

POPE'S G.S.

Well, it's hard to get information, so I'm not sure, but it's said that they target Uyghurs and Falun Gong members to harvest organs for use in organ transplants. I heard about that, and if it's true, then very inhumane things are being done.

C

That's right. It's happening in Uyghur too. They are already brainwashing and repressing millions of their people.

POPE'S G.S.

Yeah... You make stern comments because you are strong. We need people like you too.

C

Those who can express their opinions need to... I don't blame those who are really in trouble to only think about surviving, but I also think that things will never improve unless people who can express their opinions speak out. People are actually being persecuted.

POPE'S G.S.

Hmm... I'm not sure how much Master Okawa can accomplish. But I heard he can gather about as many people as I can.

"God would not be pleased with China's religious oppression and brainwashing"

C

You visited the Tokyo Dome, right.

POPE'S G.S.

Yes. But I just hold Mass and perform formalities. So, I'm not gathering people through my own personal ability. I'm just a servant of servants. Just a servant of Christianity.

Whether missionary work with an army is good or bad is very difficult to judge historically. In some ways, communism may also seem to represent Christian political opinions. It's a difficult issue. However, I cannot forgive them if they're saying, "We suppress religions because they are 'the opium of the masses.'" And if they say, "We'll brainwash every Hongkonger because they resisted, as well as every Uyghur because they are Muslim," I don't have enough right to judge Islam, but I don't think God will be pleased.

C
Hmm... It is easier to kill humans if you are materialistic.

POPE'S G.S.
Indeed.

C
When a person with mighty greed stands on top.

POPE'S G.S.
Indeed. They must be thinking, "We will let people survive as long as we have food, and we can just kill them if it runs out." If there were a war, in most cases, it would be a war

for food and resources. So, maybe Master Okawa is the only one who can fight now. There may be no one else who can judge right or wrong in regard to both spiritual and worldly aspects.

Affirmation of the spread of Master Okawa's teachings

C
I think that Jesus has a Heavenly Father.

POPE'S G.S.
Oh, yes.

C
Islam also has Allah... Allah means "God," so Elohim*...

POPE'S G.S.
At that point, you have gone far beyond my perception, so I don't really know.

* One of the core consciousnesses of El Cantare, the Supreme God of the Earth's spirit group. About 150 million years ago, Elohim descended very close to the present-day Middle East and provided wisdom with a focus on teaching the difference between light and darkness, or good and evil. See Ryuho Okawa, *The Laws of Faith: One World Beyond Differences* (New York: IRH Press, 2018).

C

But now, if you look at the situation in the world and listen to Trump's subconscious opinions (his guardian spirit's opinion), I get the strong feeling that there will never be an end to war unless people realize that, when you trace back the origins of Islam and Christianity, they come from one God.

POPE'S G.S.

Hmm... well, that is nice. It is good that Master Okawa's teachings are spreading to the U.S., Canada, Hong Kong, Taiwan, the Uyghur region, Iran, and many other places. He is doing what we cannot.

The direction in which the guardian spirit of Pope Francis wants people to think

POPE'S G.S.

The scope of my perceptions is narrow. The Vatican runs on a pretty old system. The imperial system in Japan has no real power either, right? They don't receive messages from gods and issue orders, right?

C

Unless they are careful, the Japanese imperial family may gradually be entering a world in which faith is no longer understood.

POPE'S G.S.

I'm old and I don't have much longer to live, so I don't really know. I have no choice but to leave the rest to you. But, when you are not sure what is right, I would appreciate it if you would think in the direction of bringing comfort to the weak, the troubled, the persecuted, and those who only have a limited amount of time to live.

Regarding Iran, it is not easy to determine which is less acceptable, the killing of the commander, or the government that is suppressing its citizens and women. I don't know if the U.S. has the right to devastate the Middle East.

Opinions on LGBT

C

What is your standpoint on LGBT identities? Do you accept it?

POPE'S G.S.

Oh, well, I think those who are persecuted need to be defended as much as possible until we know the outcome.

C

It is not good if people go so far as to persecute them.

POPE'S G.S.

Yet, I do not know if we should accept it as a positive right.

C

OK, I see.

POPE'S G.S.

The basic stance of the Catholic Church is that people should get married, have children, and take care of the home. So, I'm not sure. In terms of LGBT, Iran is probably its strongest enemy.

C

Well, that's right.

POPE'S G.S.

Probably.

5

Past Life, Middle East Problems, and Views on President Trump

"A long time ago, I came to Japan as a missionary and was caught"

C

Pope Francis, your soul has always been a Christian, so I am guessing that you do not know much about reincarnation.

POPE'S G.S.

I'm really at the very bottom of the pyramid.

C

No, no...

POPE'S G.S.

It is possible that I have been a mere Christian in the corner, but I don't know anything much.

C

You probably have the deepest relationship with Christianity.

POPE'S G.S.
Well, that may be the case considering my current job, but the great Christian figures of the past were all fishermen, prostitutes, tax collectors, and so on.

C
How about in Japan, none?

POPE'S G.S.
What?

C
Were you ever born in Japan?

POPE'S G.S.
Japan?

C
You speak Japanese fairly well.

POPE'S G.S.
You say this is good?

C

You're very good.

POPE'S G.S.

Thank you.

C

I'm glad that you do.

POPE'S G.S.

Hmm, I came to Japan a long, long time ago. Once upon a time, I came as a missionary and was caught.

I conveyed teachings to wartime feudal lords in Kyushu and made them Christian

C

So, does that mean you were really in the islands of Nagasaki?

POPE'S G.S.

Hmm... Maybe not just Nagasaki.

C

Was it during the Edo period?

POPE'S G.S.

I have memories of helping create many wartime feudal lords.

C

Creating many wartime feudal lords?

POPE'S G.S.

Oh no, not simply wartime feudal lords but rather Christian feudal lords.

C

Yes I see.

POPE'S G.S.

I created them in the Kyushu area. For example, people like Sorin Otomo (1530-1587).

C

Hmm?

POPE'S G.S.
Sorin Otomo.

C
Oh, I see!

POPE'S G.S.
I created people like that.

C
In other words, you conveyed Christian teachings to them?

POPE'S G.S.
Yes, to the people of Kyushu, I taught "governors" in the area and made them Christian.

C
I see.

POPE'S G.S.
If you research it, you could probably find the priest's name.

C
The person who taught them?

POPE'S G.S.

Yes, it should come up. The priest's name, at least.

"I came to Japan under the name of Rodrigues with Xavier"

C

[*About five seconds of silence.*] So, you were really with Francis Xavier and others.

POPE'S G.S.

I guess so.

C

[*About five seconds of silence.*] Was Xavier* the reincarnation of St. Paul?

POPE'S G.S.

Yes, he was a great man.

* In an earlier spiritual interview, Shiro Amakusa's spirit revealed that, in a past life, Francis Xavier, who spread Christianity to Japan, was St. Paul. See Ryuho Okawa, *Hong Kong Revolution -Spiritual messages of the guardian spirits of Xi Jinping and Agnes Chow Ting-* (Tokyo: HS Press, 2019).

C

Then, you came and worked with him.

POPE'S G.S.

I was a mere luggage bearer.

C

No, no.

POPE'S G.S.

I was just a cross-bearer.

But I did teach the feudal lords.

C

Oh, really?

POPE'S G.S.

Yes, I did. So, I studied Japanese a little...

C

You're good at it.

POPE'S G.S.

But many followers were killed too.

C
Hmm, I see. Well, you really have had a lot of painful experiences.

POPE'S G.S.
[*Exhales.*] [*About five seconds of silence.*] I'm hearing the name Rodrigues, or something like that.

C
Ah, Rodrigues?

POPE'S G.S.
It's a very common name. I don't know who it is, but I can faintly hear that name.

Opinions about becoming the pope

C
Before you became the pope, you were initially thinking of renouncing your position. Just as you were reserving your plane ticket to go to the Vatican to inform them, the Vatican summoned you.

POPE'S G.S.

The former (pope) was quite the politician. In the movie, he was played by that famous actor...

C

Anthony Hopkins.

POPE'S G.S.

Yes, he was a politician. He realized that, if I were to quit, it would look like the Vatican were crumbling or like a dissent, so he tried to win me over. After all, there were many scandals such as extravagant spending and sexual problems. So, they wanted to protect the Vatican by bringing in someone completely the opposite. He had more political power than I do, though. And the one before him had even more power.

C

Oh, I see.

POPE'S G.S.

Pope John Paul II had great power.

C
Yes, that's right.

The guardian spirit of Pope Francis remains consistently humble

C
[*About five seconds of silence.*] Was your name when you came to Japan to convey the teachings, João Tçuzu Rodrigues?

POPE'S G.S.
Well, Rodrigues is a common name, equivalent to Taro or Jiro in Japan.

C
[*Laughs.*] Yes. [*About 10 seconds of silence.*] But today, you are (in spiritual form) inside the Heavenly Father...

POPE'S G.S.
Oh, is that so?

C
Yes.

POPE'S G.S.

I have such low awareness; I'm not even sure where I am inside this 800-meter, or one-kilometer building.

C

You were probably a disciple of Xavier?

POPE'S G.S.

Well, I'm more like a porter.

C

[*Laughs.*] I see.

POPE'S G.S.

I meant, laborer. I studied Japanese a little for missionary work, and I usually just talked about Deus (God).

Thoughts on Muslims and Catholics

C

Well, I'm glad to hear that the pope is always thinking about the people around the world who are in sorrow.

POPE'S G.S.

When it comes to the people of Iran and Iraq, I do not know much about their faith, but I wish to choose the path that will bring them the least amount of suffering. And I believe it would not be easy to change a religion that has lasted for well over a millennium within a presidential term of just four or eight years. If their faith were not in accordance with God's teachings, it would have deteriorated. So, the fact that it still exists means there must be some salvation within it.

C

Yes, in the range of hundreds of millions.

POPE'S G.S.

I'm not sure about that. The Catholic Church says around one billion too. But I cannot tell how many people truly believe, though. Or, as you say, it may be that rotting bacteria are spreading within the Catholic Church. The things that Muslims hate are mostly things that are popular under Catholic regions.

Views on Israel and President Trump

C

How do you see Israel?

POPE'S G.S.

Well, there was an unhappy past. The former pope was from Germany. It's true that they needed help, but if they go to the extent of killing all the Arabs on behalf of the U.S., then that will be going too far. It would create a lot of new refugees. Arabs are going to face difficulties regarding oil soon.

They need to strive to ensure that they will be able to make a living with industries other than oil. If Iran can no longer sell oil, it will only have dates left. This is sad. They need more industries.

C

Dates seem pretty important to Japanese people because it is used in okonomiyaki sauce...

POPE'S G.S.

That's a little sad. It may be important, but you can find a substitute.

C

That's right.

POPE'S G.S.

You can live without it.

C

Yes.

POPE'S G.S.

The product may be a best match for it but, if it becomes unavailable and is substituted by something else, their profit will be zero. Mr. Trump is very good at starving strategies. He will shake their economy. I hope he is successful because it would be terrible if it were to destroy the world. That's my only worry. I want Master Okawa to keep a close eye on that.

C

Mr. Trump must be a Christian too. Dr. Peale*...

---

* President Trump followed Pastor Norman Vincent Peale, who is renowned for his book *The Power of Positive Thinking*, and according to spiritual readings conducted by Happy Science, the spirit of Pastor Peale serves as a guiding spirit for President Trump and has a religious influence.

POPE'S G.S.
He's like a half-Jewish Christian.

C
I see.

POPE'S G.S.
He's being influenced by his daughter and her husband.

C
It seems like it hasn't just been his daughter and her husband. According to Trump's guardian spirit, they haven't seemed to say much. It's probably his own...

POPE'S G.S.
Dr. Peale's Christianity is a bit heretical from the perspective of Christianity as a whole. There aren't many supporters. I think there are about one to two million in the U.S. Well, I guess it's about creating the mentality of people who succeed in business. We do not really understand that. We don't know how to make money. However, I am thankful for donations from wealthy Christians. Yet, I don't think it would be good for us to become so wealthy that we become unable to understand the feelings of the poor.

C
That's true.

St. Francis of Assisi and St. Clare of Assisi are far greater

C
I am sure that, as the pope, you pray.

POPE'S G.S.
Yes.

C
Do you have a guiding spirit? Someone that connects with you spiritually and gives you advice?

POPE'S G.S.
To me, St. Francis of Assisi seems as high up as the top of Mt. Everest, so the only spirits around me are the ghosts of Vatican residents.

C
No, no [*laughs*]. So, not even St. Clare of Assisi*?

POPE'S G.S.

You brought up a great name. For us, she looks like the next in line to Mother Mary.

She is not someone that we could ever approach. That would be impossible. She is much greater than me.

C

I understand.

* St. Clare of Assisi (1194-1253): An Italian saint. She was born into a wealthy family, but she became one of the first followers of Francis of Assisi. She founded the Order of Poor Ladies, a monastic religious order.

6
Message for Japanese People

"I want Japanese people to help people around the world a little more"

C

Then finally, although you (Pope Francis) did come to Japan not long ago, since you are giving us this message in Japanese, can you please give a message to the Japanese people as the guardian spirit of pope?

POPE'S G.S.

Well, I hear that Japan is a little stagnant as a nation, and there are indications of deterioration, but from the point of view of places around the world like Latin America, Africa, and Central Asia, Japan has been successful in realizing an outstanding and affluent lifestyle and in creating a peaceful nation. So, please stop refusing to accept immigrants and stop worrying about population decline. You should accept more immigrants who are good people and who believe in God or Buddha. Japan could probably accommodate about 200 million people. Japan's agriculture has weakened, its fishing has weakened, and there are fewer people who can till the fields.

You can accept more of these people and allow them to acquire skills so they can go back to their home country to build up their own nation. I think you may be able to incorporate such policies. It would make me happy if you took on that obligation. America did it to some extent, didn't it? So did the U.K. Japan only accepts around 200 immigrants* a year. This does not meet world demand at all.

If tens of thousands of people were to actually acquire skills, knowledge, and education over a period of several years in Japan, and they can learn how to start new industries and how to manage factories, then they may be able to start industries in their own countries, which will free many people from poverty. That's why I want you to think about helping people around the world a little more. Even if you're not a Christian nation, it would make me happy if you felt that way. That's my hope.

C

I understand. You want Japan to think more about the world.

---

* In April 2019, the category of "Specified Skilled Worker" was established as a new residency status to expand the employment of foreigners in Japan. In November 2019, the Japanese government announced that there were 219 foreign residents possessing the status of "Specified Skilled Worker." The number has since been increasing.

POPE'S G.S.
Yes, yes. You seem too worried about the population decline, but there are many people who wish to go to Japan. You should let them in. You should ask them to study Japanese and let them in. That's what I think.

C
I understand.

Independent decision-making regarding Japanese interests

POPE'S G.S.
The Japanese are religiously vague, but I think they are highly-moral citizens.

C
I don't think Japanese people are very prejudiced toward or think badly of people who follow world religions.

POPE'S G.S.
Well, if an emergency situation develops in somewhere like Hong Kong or Taiwan, I want Japan to make an effort to

accept the people. In the future, there may be various battles fought in the Philippines, Malaysia, and other places. Also, I think it's better to be friendly with Russia if possible.

Mr. Trump is resolute, so Russia is very cautious about the Japan-U.S. alliance, and it would be hard to enter into a Japan-Russia peace treaty. But Japan should have its own stance.

Japan refused to join the coalition of the willing and only sent the Self-Defense Force to the Gulf region to conduct investigations and research, and Mr. Abe visited three oil-producing countries, right? That's an independent stance. So, it should be fine to take an independent position regarding Russia too.

C

Japan can have its own relationship with Russia, and...

POPE'S G.S.

That's right. Japan doesn't need to be on board with America's conflicts. Japan should independently make decisions about its own interests. Russia doesn't really have the strength to fight with the U.S. right now. It is now trying to rebuild from its previous collapse.

What to do with North Korea and South Korea is a

problem, but I think Japan must divide responsibility for this issue evenly with the U.S. It's about the relationships between China, North Korea, and South Korea.

In South Korea, although Christianity is influential, they have to change a little. I want to do something, but I haven't been successful. I look forward to your efforts.

"I see Happy Science as a hopeful religion"

C

There's just one more question. We are all, except Master, religious practitioners, so do you have any advice from the standpoint of religious leaders?

POPE'S G.S.

Well, you seem to be splendid people.

While we are studying the Bible and Latin, you seem to be learning the structure of contemporary society and engaging in other studies, and merging them with religion. So, I think you are a very hopeful religion. In terms of time, I probably won't be able to witness everything, but I hope you become a grand religion capable of having great influence and pulling the world in a positive direction. I do not have the words to persuade powerful people like Mr. Trump, Mr. Putin, Mr. Khamenei, and Mr. Xi Jinping, so I hope that you will be able to generate persuasive words and communicate with them.

Anyway, I think you are a hopeful religion, and that's good. What we can only imagine it as a happening from 2,000 years ago, you are able to understand right now, aren't you?

C
Well, the only reason that we understand which direction to go is that Master Ryuho Okawa teaches us.

POPE'S G.S.
We can imagine what Jesus was like 2,000 years ago, and interpret things through writings. But as ordinary people, we can only imagine what Jesus would do if he were here today.

C
I think that most people with faith wonder what God would say in different situations, and right now is a miraculous time in which we are being given the answers to what we want to ask God.

"Even the pope can't receive answers from Jesus in his prayers" "Please take care of the people of the world hereafter"

POPE'S G.S.
Even though I have been elected to the position of the pope, I can't receive answers from Jesus in my prayers. Not once. So, if Master Okawa prays, despite not being a Christian, and Jesus answers, that is probably something extraordinary. I don't know much about it, but if he concentrates on Islam, prays to Allah, and understands Allah's thoughts, then that is something extraordinary. I do not deny that such things might happen. I think it's possible. Since you're in the East, I think that Buddha may even appear. If we are living in such a splendid era, then I want to witness such great power. But at any rate, I'm already old, so please take care of the people of the world hereafter. Thank you.

C
Thank you very much.

POPE'S G.S.
Yes.

Afterword

My goal was to shed light on how the current coronavirus pandemic is seen in the Spirit World, while at the same time contrasting the ideas of Jesus Christ, who is now a spiritual being, with the ideas of the guardian spirit of the currently reigning pope.

Part One, Chapter One draws attention to the differences between the guardian spirit's opinion and those of other high spirits conveyed by Happy Science. Part Two presents the calm, sober views of the pope's guardian spirit as of January 2020.

My prediction is that the coronavirus pandemic will not die down within one or two months, and that people will likely have to learn to coexist with this coronavirus.

Instead of relying on your government for survival, the proper course of action is to pull through this by doing what you can on your own. Although we might be facing a possible war, we should prevent the establishment of despotism and totalitarianism, and cherish freedom, human rights, and the fact that we are independent (not being enslaved).

Also, putting aside Pope Francis's feelings of powerlessness, people must strengthen their belief in the True God.

Ryuho Okawa
Master & CEO of Happy Science Group
May 1, 2020

ABOUT THE AUTHOR

RYUHO OKAWA was born on July 7th 1956, in Tokushima, Japan. After graduating from the University of Tokyo with a law degree, he joined a Tokyo-based trading house. While working at its New York headquarters, he studied international finance at the Graduate Center of the City University of New York. In 1981, he attained Great Enlightenment and became aware that he is El Cantare with a mission to bring salvation to all of humankind. In 1986, he established Happy Science. It now has members in over 100 countries across the world, with more than 700 local branches and temples as well as 10,000 missionary houses around the world. The total number of lectures has exceeded 3,150 (of which more than 150 are in English) and over 2,700 books (of which more than 550 are Spiritual Interview Series) have been published, many of which are translated into 31 languages. Many of the books, including *The Laws of the Sun* have become best sellers or million sellers. To date, Happy Science has produced 20 movies. The original story and original concept were given by the Executive Producer Ryuho Okawa. Recent movie titles are *The Real Exorcist* (live-action, May 2020), *Living in the Age of Miracles* (documentary scheduled to be released in Aug. 2020), and *Twiceborn* (live-action, scheduled to be released in Oct. 2020). He has also composed the lyrics and music of over 100 songs, such as theme songs and featured songs of movies. Moreover, he is the Founder of Happy Science University and Happy Science Academy (Junior and Senior High School), Founder and President of the Happiness Realization Party, Founder and Honorary Headmaster of Happy Science Institute of Government and Management, Founder of IRH Press Co., Ltd., and the Chairperson of New Star Production Co., Ltd. and ARI Production Co., Ltd.

WHAT IS EL CANTARE?

El Cantare means "the Light of the Earth," and is the Supreme God of the Earth who has been guiding humankind since the beginning of Genesis. He is whom Jesus called Father and Muhammad called Allah. Different parts of El Cantare's core consciousness have descended to Earth in the past, once as Alpha and another as Elohim. His branch spirits, such as Shakyamuni Buddha and Hermes, have descended to Earth many times and helped to flourish many civilizations. To unite various religions and to integrate various fields of study in order to build a new civilization on Earth, a part of the core consciousness has descended to Earth as Master Ryuho Okawa.

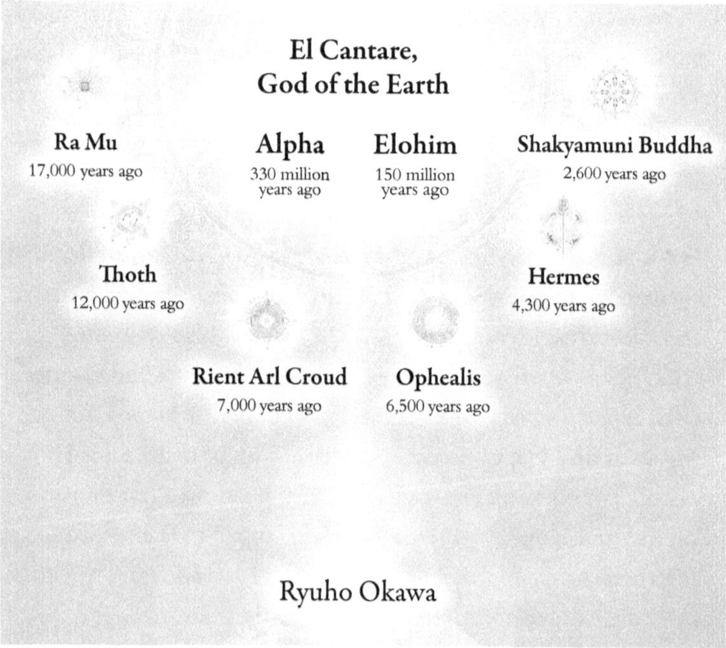

Alpha is a part of the core consciousness of El Cantare who descended to Earth around 330 million years ago. Alpha preached Earth's Truths to harmonize and unify Earth-born humans and space people who came from other planets.

Elohim is a part of El Cantare's core consciousness who descended to Earth around 150 million years ago. He gave wisdom, mainly on the differences of light and darkness, good and evil.

Shakyamuni Buddha was born as a prince into the Shakya Clan in India around 2,600 years ago. When he was 29 years old, he renounced the world and sought enlightenment. He later attained Great Enlightenment and founded Buddhism.

Hermes is one of the 12 Olympian gods in Greek mythology, but the spiritual Truth is that he taught the teachings of love and progress around 4,300 years ago that became the origin of the current Western civilization. He is a hero that truly existed.

Ophealis was born in Greece around 6,500 years ago and was the leader who took an expedition to as far as Egypt. He is the God of miracles, prosperity, and arts, and is known as Osiris in the Egyptian mythology.

Rient Arl Croud was born as a king of the ancient Incan Empire around 7,000 years ago and taught about the mysteries of the mind. In the heavenly world, he is responsible for the interactions that take place between various planets.

Thoth was an almighty leader who built the golden age of the Atlantic civilization around 12,000 years ago. In the Egyptian mythology, he is known as god Thoth.

Ra Mu was a leader who built the golden age of the civilization of Mu around 17,000 years ago. As a religious leader and a politician, he ruled by uniting religion and politics.

WHAT IS A SPIRITUAL MESSAGE?

We are all spiritual beings living on this earth. The following is the mechanism behind Master Ryuho Okawa's spiritual messages.

1 You are a spirit

People are born into this world to gain wisdom through various experiences and return to the other world when their lives end. We are all spirits and repeat this cycle in order to refine our souls.

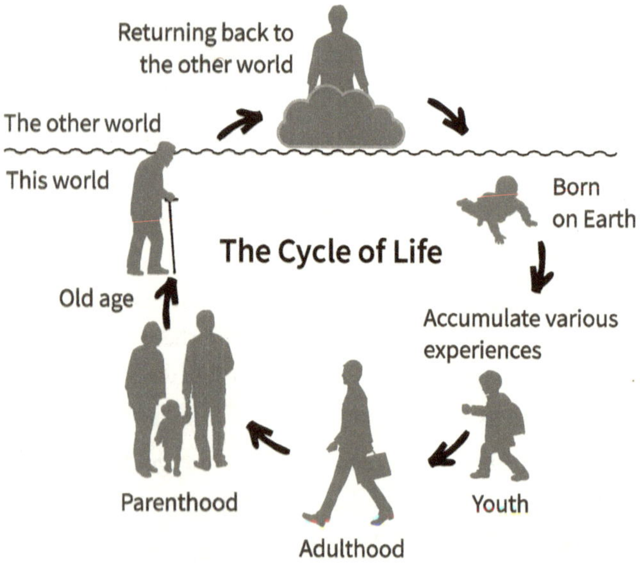

2 You have a guardian spirit

Guardian spirits are those who protect the people who are living on this earth. Each of us has a guardian spirit that watches over us and guides us from the other world. They were us in our past life, and are identical in how we think.

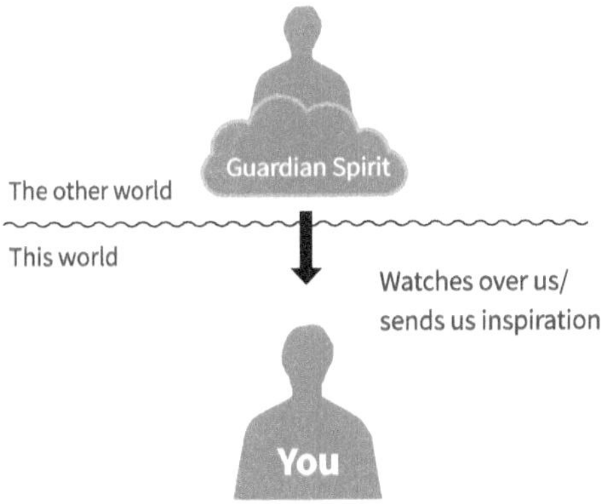

3 How spiritual messages work

Master Ryuho Okawa, through his enlightenment, is capable of summoning any spirit from anywhere in the world, including the spirit world.

Master Okawa's way of receiving spiritual messages is fundamentally different from that of other psychic mediums who undergo trances and are thereby completely taken over by the spirits they are channeling.

Master Okawa's attainment of a high level of enlightenment enables him to retain full control of his consciousness and body throughout the duration of the spiritual message. To allow the spirits to express their own thoughts and personalities freely, however, Master Okawa usually softens the dominancy of his consciousness. This way, he is able to keep his own philosophies out of the way and ensure that the spiritual messages are pure expressions of the spirits he is channeling.

Since guardian spirits think at the same subconscious level as the person living on earth, Master Okawa can summon the spirit and find out what the person on earth is actually thinking. If the person has already returned to the other world, the spirit can give messages to the people living on earth through Master Okawa.

Since 2009, more than 1,050 sessions of spiritual messages have been openly recorded by Master Okawa, and the majority of these have been published. Spiritual messages from the guardian spirits of people living today such as Donald Trump, Japanese Prime Minister Shinzo Abe and Chinese President Xi Jinping, as well as spiritual messages sent from the spirit world by Jesus Christ, Muhammad, Thomas Edison, Mother Teresa, Steve Jobs and Nelson Mandela are just a tiny pack of spiritual messages that were published so far.

Domestically, in Japan, these spiritual messages are being read by a wide range of politicians and mass media, and the high-level contents of these books are delivering an impact even more on politics, news and public opinion. In recent years, there have been spiritual messages recorded in English, and English translations are being done on the spiritual messages given in Japanese. These have been published overseas, one after another, and have started to shake the world.

...
1 The guardian spirit / spirit in the other world...
...
2 Goes inside Master Okawa in this world
3 Master Okawa speaks the words of the guardian spirit / spirit

For more about spiritual messages and a complete list of books in the Spiritual Interview Series, visit ***okawabooks.com***

ABOUT HAPPY SCIENCE

Happy Science is a global movement that empowers individuals to find purpose and spiritual happiness and to share that happiness with their families, societies, and the world. With more than twelve million members around the world, Happy Science aims to increase awareness of spiritual truths and expand our capacity for love, compassion, and joy so that together we can create the kind of world we all wish to live in.

Activities at Happy Science are based on the Principles of Happiness (Love, Wisdom, Self-Reflection, and Progress). These principles embrace worldwide philosophies and beliefs, transcending boundaries of culture and religions.

Love teaches us to give ourselves freely without expecting anything in return; it encompasses giving, nurturing, and forgiving.

Wisdom leads us to the insights of spiritual truths, and opens us to the true meaning of life and the will of God (the universe, the highest power, Buddha).

Self-Reflection brings a mindful, nonjudgmental lens to our thoughts and actions to help us find our truest selves—the essence of our souls—and deepen our connection to the highest power. It helps us attain a clean and peaceful mind and leads us to the right life path.

Progress emphasizes the positive, dynamic aspects of our spiritual growth—actions we can take to manifest and spread happiness around the world. It's a path that not only expands our soul growth, but also furthers the collective potential of the world we live in.

PROGRAMS AND EVENTS

The doors of Happy Science are open to all. We offer a variety of programs and events, including self-exploration and self-growth programs, spiritual seminars, meditation and contemplation sessions, study groups, and book events.

Our programs are designed to:

* Deepen your understanding of your purpose and meaning in life
* Improve your relationships and increase your capacity to love unconditionally
* Attain peace of mind, decrease anxiety and stress, and feel positive
* Gain deeper insights and a broader perspective on the world
* Learn how to overcome life's challenges

... and much more.

*For more information, visit **happy-science.org**.*

OUR ACTIVITIES

Happy Science does other various activities to provide support for those in need.

- **You Are An Angel! General Incorporated Association**

  Happy Science has a volunteer network in Japan that encourages and supports children with disabilities as well as their parents and guardians.

- **Never Mind School for Truancy**

  At 'Never Mind,' we support students who find it very challenging to attend schools in Japan. We also nurture their self-help spirit and power to rebound against obstacles in life based on Master Okawa's teachings and faith.

- **"Prevention Against Suicide" Campaign since 2003**

  A nationwide campaign to reduce suicides; over 20,000 people commit suicide every year in Japan. "The Suicide Prevention Website-Words of Truth for You-" presents spiritual prescriptions for worries such as depression, lost love, extramarital affairs, bullying and work-related problems, thereby saving many lives.

- **Support for Anti-bullying Campaigns**

  Happy Science provides support for a group of parents and guardians, Network to Protect Children from Bullying, a general incorporated foundation launched in Japan to end bullying, including those that can even be called a criminal offense. So far, the network received more than 5,000 cases and resolved 90% of them.

◆ **The Golden Age Scholarship**

This scholarship is granted to students who can contribute greatly and bring a hopeful future to the world.

◆ **Success No.1**
Buddha's Truth Afterschool Academy

Happy Science has over 180 classrooms throughout Japan and in several cities around the world that focus on afterschool education for children. The education focuses on faith and morals in addition to supporting children's school studies.

◆ **Angel Plan V**

For children under the age of kindergarten, Happy Science holds classes for nurturing healthy, positive, and creative boys and girls.

◆ **Future Stars Training Department**

The Future Stars Training Department was founded within the Happy Science Media Division with the goal of nurturing talented individuals to become successful in the performing arts and entertainment industry.

◆ **New Star Production Co., Ltd.**
ARI Production Co., Ltd.

We have companies to nurture actors and actresses, artists, and vocalists. They are also involved in film production.

DOCUMENTARY MOVIE
HEART TO HEART

In this documentary movie, Happy Science University students visit these NPO activities to discover what salvation truly is, and on the meaning of life, through heart-to-heart interviews.

ABOUT HAPPY SCIENCE MOVIES

LIVING IN THE AGE OF MIRACLES

A documentary film to be released in Aug. 2020

An inspirational documentary about two Japanese actors meeting people who experienced miracles in their lives. Through their quest, they find the key to working miracles and learn what "living in the age of miracles" truly means.

GOLD AWARD
Documentary Feature
International
Independent Film Awards
Spring 2020

GOLD AWARD
Concept
International
Independent Film Awards
Spring 2020

THE REAL EXORCIST

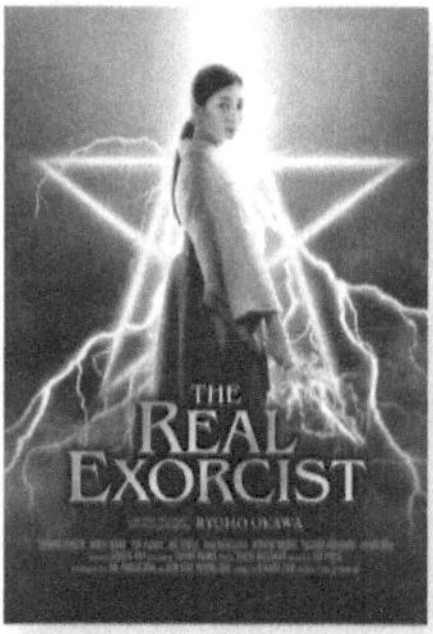

46 Awards from 7 Countries!

STORY Tokyo —the most mystical city in the world where you find spiritual spots in the most unexpected places. Sayuri works as a part time waitress at a small coffee shop "Extra" where regular customers enjoy the authentic coffee that the owner brews. Meanwhile, Sayuri uses her supernatural powers to help those who are troubled by spiritual phenomena one after another. Through her special consultations, she touches the hearts of the people and helps them by showing the truths of the invisible world.

USA

GOLD REMI AWARD
53rd WorldFest Houston
International Film Festival 2020

NIGERIA

BEST FEATURE FILM
EKO International Film Festival
2020

BEST SUPPORTING ACTRESS
EKO International Film Festival
2020

MONACO

BEST FEATURE FILM
17th Angel Film Awards
2020
Monaco International Film Festival

BEST FEMALE ACTOR
17th Angel Film Awards
2020
Monaco International Film Festival

BEST FEMALE SUPPORTING ACTOR
17th Angel Film Awards
2020
Monaco International Film Festival

BEST VISUAL EFFECTS
17th Angel Film Awards
2020
Monaco International Film Festival

...and more!

For more information, visit **www.realexorcistmovie.com**

IMMORTAL HERO On VOD NOW

Based on the true story of a man whose near death experience inspires him to choose life... and change the lives of millions.

38 Awards from 9 Countries!

SPAIN
BARCELONA INTERNATIONAL FILM FESTIVAL 2019 [THE CASTELL AWARDS]

SPAIN
MADRID INTERNATIONAL FILM FESTIVAL 2019 [BEST DIRECTOR OF A FOREIGN LANGUAGE FEATURE FILM]

ITALY
FLORENCE FILM AWARDS JUL 2019 [HONORABLE MENTION: FEATURE FILM]

USA
INDIE VISIONS FILM FESTIVAL JUL 2019 [WINNER (NARRATIVE FEATURE FILM)]

ITALY
FLORENCE FILM AWARDS JUL 2019 [BEST ORIGINAL SCREENPLAY]

ITALY
DIAMOND FILM AWARDS JUL 2019 [WINNER (NARRATIVE FEATUREFILM)]

...and more!

For more information, visit ***www.immortal-hero.com***

Animation

THE LAWS OF THE UNIVERSE - PART I

Battle requires strength. Harmony requires even more.

7 Awards from 4 Countries!

FRANCE
NICE INTERNATIONAL FILM FESTIVAL 2019 BEST INTERNATIONAL ANIMATION AWARD

UK
LONDON INTERNATIONAL MOTION PICTURE AWARDS 2019 BEST INTERNATIONAL ANIMATION FEATURE FILM AWARD

USA
AWARENESS FILM FESTIVAL [SPECIAL JURY ANIMATION AWARD]

USA
FILM INVASION LOS ANGELES [GRAND JURY PRIZE – BEST ANIME FEATURE]

...and more!

For more information, visit ***https://laws-of-universe.hspicturesstudio.com/***

Documentary

LIFE IS BEAUTIFUL

Six people seeking their purposes of life

BRONZE REMI AWARD
53rd WORLDFEST HOUSTON INTERNATIONAL FILM FESTIVAL 2020

CONTACT INFORMATION

Happy Science is a worldwide organization with faith centers around the globe. For a comprehensive list of centers, visit the worldwide directory at ***happy-science.org***. The following are some of the many Happy Science locations:

UNITED STATES AND CANADA

New York
79 Franklin St., New York, NY 10013
Phone: 212-343-7972
Fax: 212-343-7973
Email: ny@happy-science.org
Website: happyscience-na.org

New Jersey
725 River Rd, #102B, Edgewater, NJ 07020
Phone: 201-313-0127
Fax: 201-313-0120
Email: nj@happy-science.org
Website: happyscience-na.org

Florida
5208 8th St., St. Zephyrhills, FL 33542
Phone: 813-715-0000
Fax: 813-715-0010
Email: florida@happy-science.org
Website: happyscience-na.org

Atlanta
1874 Piedmont Ave., NE Suite 360-C
Atlanta, GA 30324
Phone: 404-892-7770
Email: atlanta@happy-science.org
Website: happyscience-na.org

San Francisco
525 Clinton St.
Redwood City, CA 94062
Phone & Fax: 650-363-2777
Email: sf@happy-science.org
Website: happyscience-na.org

Los Angeles
1590 E. Del Mar Blvd., Pasadena, CA 91106
Phone: 626-395-7775
Fax: 626-395-7776
Email: la@happy-science.org
Website: happyscience-na.org

Orange County
10231 Slater Ave., #204
Fountain Valley, CA 92708
Phone: 714-745-1140
Email: oc@happy-science.org
Website: happyscience-na.org

San Diego
7841 Balboa Ave., Suite #202
San Diego, CA 92111
Phone: 619-381-7615
Fax: 626-395-7776
E-mail: sandiego@happy-science.org
Website: happyscience-na.org

Hawaii
Phone: 808-591-9772
Fax: 808-591-9776
Email: hi@happy-science.org
Website: happyscience-na.org

Kauai
3343 Kanakolu Street, Suite 5
Lihue, HI 96766, U.S.A.
Phone: 808-822-7007
Fax: 808-822-6007
Email: kauai-hi@happy-science.org
Website: kauai.happyscience-na.org

Toronto
845 The Queensway
Etobicoke ON M8Z 1N6 Canada
Phone: 1-416-901-3747
Email: toronto@happy-science.org
Website: happy-science.ca

Vancouver
#201-2607 East 49th Avenue
Vancouver, BC, V5S 1J9, Canada
Phone: 1-604-437-7735
Fax: 1-604-437-7764
Email: vancouver@happy-science.org
Website: happy-science.ca

INTERNATIONAL

Tokyo
1-6-7 Togoshi, Shinagawa
Tokyo, 142-0041 Japan
Phone: 81-3-6384-5770
Fax: 81-3-6384-5776
Email: tokyo@happy-science.org
Website: happy-science.org

Seoul
74, Sadang-ro 27-gil,
Dongjak-gu, Seoul, Korea
Phone: 82-2-3478-8777
Fax: 82-2-3478-9777
Email: korea@happy-science.org
Website: happyscience-korea.org

London
3 Margaret St.
London,W1W 8RE United Kingdom
Phone: 44-20-7323-9255
Fax: 44-20-7323-9344
Email: eu@happy-science.org
Website: happyscience-uk.org

Taipei
No. 89, Lane 155, Dunhua N. Road
Songshan District, Taipei City 105, Taiwan
Phone: 886-2-2719-9377
Fax: 886-2-2719-5570
Email: taiwan@happy-science.org
Website: happyscience-tw.org

Sydney
516 Pacific Hwy, Lane Cove North,
NSW 2066, Australia
Phone: 61-2-9411-2877
Fax: 61-2-9411-2822
Email: sydney@happy-science.org

Malaysia
No 22A, Block 2, Jalil Link Jalan Jalil Jaya 2,
Bukit Jalil 57000, Kuala Lumpur, Malaysia
Phone: 60-3-8998-7877
Fax: 60-3-8998-7977
Email: malaysia@happy-science.org
Website: happyscience.org.my

Brazil Headquarters
Rua. Domingos de Morais 1154,
Vila Mariana, Sao Paulo SP
CEP 04009-002, Brazil
Phone: 55-11-5088-3800
Fax: 55-11-5088-3806
Email: sp@happy-science.org
Website: happyscience.com.br

Nepal
Kathmandu Metropolitan City Ward
No. 15,
Ring Road, Kimdol,
Sitapaila Kathmandu, Nepal
Phone: 97-714-272931
Email: nepal@happy-science.org

Jundiai
Rua Congo, 447, Jd. Bonfiglioli
Jundiai-CEP, 13207-340
Phone: 55-11-4587-5952
Email: jundiai@happy-science.org

Uganda
Plot 877 Rubaga Road, Kampala
P.O. Box 34130, Kampala, Uganda
Phone: 256-79-4682-121
Email: uganda@happy-science.org
Website: happyscience-uganda.org

ABOUT HAPPINESS REALIZATION PARTY

The Happiness Realization Party (HRP) was founded in May 2009 by Master Ryuho Okawa as part of the Happy Science Group to offer concrete and proactive solutions to the current issues such as military threats from North Korea and China and the long-term economic recession. HRP aims to implement drastic reforms of the Japanese government, thereby bringing peace and prosperity to Japan. To accomplish this, HRP proposes two key policies:

1) Strengthening the national security and the Japan-U.S. alliance, which plays a vital role in the stability of Asia.

2) Improving the Japanese economy by implementing drastic tax cuts, taking monetary easing measures and creating new major industries.

HRP advocates that Japan should offer a model of a religious nation that allows diverse values and beliefs to coexist, and that contributes to global peace.

For more information, visit **en.hr-party.jp**

ABOUT IRH PRESS

IRH Press Co., Ltd., based in Tokyo, was founded in 1987 as a publishing division of Happy Science. IRH Press publishes religious and spiritual books, journals, magazines and also operates broadcast and film production enterprises. For more information, visit *okawabooks.com*.

Follow us on:

Facebook: Okawa Books
Goodreads: Ryuho Okawa
Pinterest: Okawa Books
Twitter: Okawa Books
Instagram: OkawaBooks

RYUHO OKAWA'S LAWS SERIES

The Laws Series is an annual volume of books that are mainly comprised of Ryuho Okawa's lectures on various topics that highlight principles and guidelines for the activities of Happy Science every year. *The Laws of the Sun*, the first publication of the Laws Series, ranked in the annual best-selling list in Japan in 1987. Since then, all of the Laws Series' titles have ranked in the annual best-selling list for more than two decades, setting sociocultural trends in Japan and around the world.

THE TRILOGY

The first three volumes of the Laws Series, *The Laws of the Sun*, *The Golden Laws*, and *The Nine Dimensions* make a trilogy that completes the basic framework of the teachings of God's Truths. *The Laws of the Sun* discusses the structure of God's Laws, *The Golden Laws* expounds on the doctrine of time, and *The Nine Dimensions* reveals the nature of space.

BOOKS BY RYUHO OKAWA

THE LAWS OF THE SUN

ONE SOURCE, ONE PLANET, ONE PEOPLE

Paperback • 288 pages • $15.95
ISBN: 978-1-942125-43-3

IMAGINE IF YOU COULD ASK GOD why He created this world and what spiritual laws He used to shape us—and everything around us. If we could understand His designs and intentions, we could discover what our goals in life should be and whether our actions move us closer to those goals or farther away.

At a young age, a spiritual calling prompted Ryuho Okawa to outline what he innately understood to be universal truths for all humankind. In *The Laws of the Sun*, Okawa outlines these laws of the universe and provides a road map for living one's life with greater purpose and meaning.

In this powerful book, Ryuho Okawa reveals the transcendent nature of consciousness and the secrets of our multidimensional universe and our place in it. By understanding the different stages of love and following the Buddhist Eightfold Path, he believes we can speed up our eternal process of development. *The Laws of the Sun* shows the way to realize true happiness—a happiness that continues from this world through the other.

For a complete list of books, visit ***okawabooks.com***

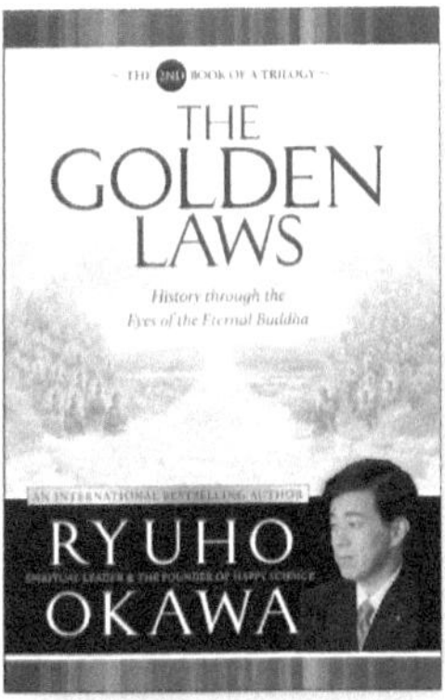

THE GOLDEN LAWS

HISTORY THROUGH THE EYES OF THE ETERNAL BUDDHA

Paperback • 201 pages • $14.95
ISBN: 978-1-941779-81-1

Throughout history, Great Guiding Spirits of Light have been present on Earth in both the East and the West at crucial points in human history to further our spiritual development. *The Golden Laws* reveals how Divine Plan has been unfolding on Earth, and outlines 5,000 years of the secret history of humankind. Once we understand the true course of history, through past, present and into the future, we cannot help but become aware of the significance of our spiritual mission in the present age.

THE NINE DIMENSIONS

UNVEILING THE LAWS OF ETERNITY

Paperback • 168 pages • $15.95
ISBN: 978-0-982698-56-3

This book is a window into the mind of our loving God, who designed this world and the vast, wondrous world of our afterlife as a school with many levels through which our souls learn and grow. When the religions and cultures of the world discover the truth of their common spiritual origin, they will be inspired to accept their differences, come together under faith in God, and build an era of harmony and peaceful progress on Earth.

The Real Exorcist

Attain Wisdom to Conquer Evil

Paperback • 208 pages • $16.95
ISBN:978-1-942125-67-9

This is a profound spiritual text backed by the author's nearly forty years of real-life experience with spiritual phenomena. In it, Okawa teaches how we may discern and overcome our negative tendencies, by acquiring the right knowledge, mindset and lifestyle.

The Laws of Steel

Living a Life of Resilience,
Confidence and Prosperity

Paperback • 256 pages • $16.95
ISBN: 978-1-942125-65-5

This book is a compilation of six lectures that Ryuho Okawa gave in 2018 and 2019, each containing passionate messages for us to open a brighter future. This powerful and inspiring book will not only show us the ways to achieve true happiness and prosperity, but also the ways to solve many global issues we now face.

Messages from Heaven

What Jesus, Buddha, Moses, and
Muhammad Would Say Today

Hardcover • 214 pages • $19.95
ISBN: 978-1-941779-19-4

If you could speak to Jesus, Buddha, Moses, or Muhammad, what would you ask? Ryuho Okawa uses his spiritual power to communicate with these four spirits and shares their messages to the people living today.

For a complete list of books, visit ***okawabooks.com***

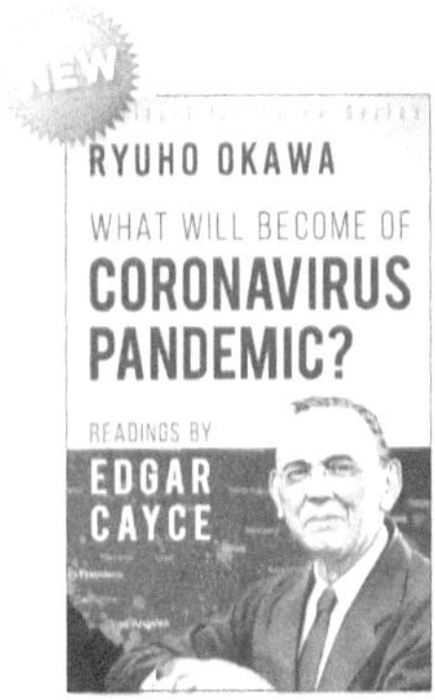

What Will Become of Coronavirus Pandemic?

Readings by Edgar Cayce

Paperback • 86 pages • $9.95
ISBN: 978-1-943869-82-4

Edgar Cayce, now a spirit in heaven, tells us that the novel coronavirus infection is likely to spread even further, but he also teaches us the truth behind it and how to deal with it. Your city may be in a lockdown, but you, yourself, can gain the power to defeat the novel coronavirus. Here is your light of hope.

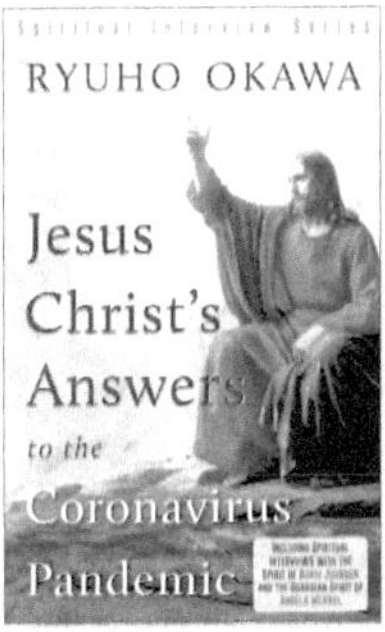

Jesus Christ's Answers to the Coronavirus Pandemic

Paperback • 204 pages • $11.95
ISBN: 978-1-943869-81-7

In this book, the spirit of Jesus answers the causes, prospects, and coping strategies for the novel coronavirus pandemic. Instead of hoping for the development of an effective vaccine to come soon, we should use our spiritual power to defeat the evil thoughts that spiritually possess this virus. It's a book for all who believe in Jesus.

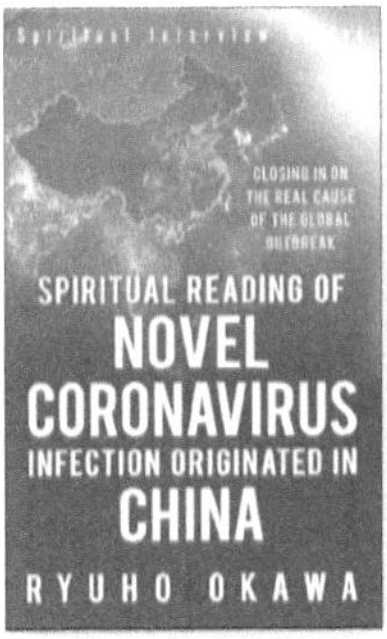

Spiritual Reading of Novel Coronavirus Infection Originated in China

Closing in on the Real Cause of the Global Outbreak

Paperback • 278 pages • $13.95
ISBN: 978-1-943869-77-0

This worldwide pandemic is not a mere act of nature nor a coincidence, but rather, heaven's warning to humanity, especially China. Through this book, you can find out "the immunity" against the novel coronavirus, among other shocking truths.

THE NEW RESURRECTION
My Miraculous Story of Overcoming Illness and Death

THE ROYAL ROAD OF LIFE
Beginning Your Path of Inner Peace, Virtue, and a Life of Purpose

THE LAWS OF GREAT ENLIGHTENMENT
Always Walk with Buddha

I CAN
Discover Your Power Within

THE HELL YOU NEVER KNEW
And How to Avoid Going There

THE LAWS OF FAITH
One World Beyond Differences

THE STARTING POINT OF HAPPINESS
An Inspiring Guide to Positive Living with Faith, Love, and Courage

HEALING FROM WITHIN
Life-Changing Keys to Calm, Spiritual, and Healthy Living

SPIRITUAL WORLD 101
A Guide to a Spiritually Happy Life

---

*For a complete list of books, visit **okawabooks.com***